24.95

WEAPONS OF THE U.S. ARMY RANGERS

RUSS AND SUSAN BRYANT

Zenith Press titles are also available at discounts in bulk quantity for industrial or sales-promotional use. For details write to Special Sales Manager at MBI Publishing Company, Galtier Plaza, Suite 200, 380 Jackson Street, St. Paul, MN 55101-3885 USA.

ISBN 0-7603-2112-4

Editorial: Steve Gansen and Lindsay Hitch
Design: Brenda Canales and Kally Lane

Printed in China

Contents

Acknowledgments

Words are not enough to express my deepest gratitude to the men of the 75th Ranger Regiment for their professionalism, brotherhood, and willingness to continually place themselves in harm's way for the security of our great nation.

Thank you to Steve Gansen, friend and editor at MBI, for his willingness to see this project come to completion and for his guidance along the way.

Thanks to the U.S. Army Special Operations Command Public Affairs Office (PAO), Carol Darby and Barbara Ashley; Bruce Zielsdorf, Chief PAO U.S. Army, and his staff; and the S-5 shops at 1st Ranger Battalion and the 75th Ranger Regiment headquarters.

A special thanks to Kimberly T. Laudano at the 75th Ranger Regiment PAO for all the e-mails and answers, and for being the only PAO officer ever to wear a Kevlar helmet and body armor and run down a live fire lane with me!

I extend my appreciation to: My awesome wife, Susan, for writing an outstanding book and being a ranger wife for four years. My family, Morgan and Travis, for being understanding and giving me time to work. My parents, Bill and Barbara Bryant, for their constant support and guidance over the years. Kevin Thompson of Velocity Works for his friendship and technical support.

Thanks to the Savannah College of Art and Design.

Thank you to Alex Gilmore at Bay Camera Company, Savannah, Georgia, for equipment support.

Background of the 75th Ranger Regiment

The greatest weapon in the global war on terrorism is still the volunteer American male who is highly disciplined, intrinsically motivated, specifically trained, and proudly wears the scroll of the 75th Ranger Regiment, whether of the 1st, 2nd, or 3rd Battalions. This elite American infantryman will accomplish and complete missions against insurmountable odds when all remaining units have declined or failed. He willingly embraces unexpected circumstances in a varied and complicated distant battlefield. With the most advanced equipment in the world and the expectation of success from the world watching, failure is not an option for the Ranger. A grateful nation asks for extraordinary things under extraordinary conditions, and the Ranger quietly and professionally answers.

The brotherhood of these exceptional warriors is bound by their unique experiences on combat missions throughout Central America, Eastern Europe, Africa, and the Middle East. Missions are readily accepted by Rangers, who, in the blink of an eye, travel to distant places such as Takur Ghar mountain, Hadithah Dam, Tora Bora mountain caves, Mogadishu, and Baghdad.

Ranger soldiers are known worldwide as the epitome of the infantryman. A Ranger is a warrior of indomitable will. He is a consummate leader who thrives on adversity and inspires total trust and confidence in his ability to do what is right in any situation. A Ranger is a uniquely qualified soldier who will fight and win anywhere in the world. As history has proven, whenever the United States is involved in a conflict, a ranger force has been and will be involved.

The 75th Ranger Regiment, composed of three ranger battalions, is the premier light-infantry unit of the United States Army. Headquartered at Fort Benning, Georgia, the 75th Ranger Regiment's mission is to plan and conduct special missions in support of the policy and objectives of the United States. The three ranger battalions that comprise the 75th Ranger Regiment are geographically dispersed. Their locations are:

- 1st Battalion, 75th Ranger Regiment, Hunter Army Airfield (Fort Stewart), Georgia
- 2nd Battalion, 75th Ranger Regiment, Fort Lewis, Washington
- 3rd Battalion, 75th Ranger Regiment, Fort Benning, Georgia

Each ranger battalion is authorized 660 personnel assigned to three rifle companies and a headquarters company. The rifle companies consist of 152 Rangers each, while the headquarters company consists of the remaining Rangers. Each rifle company within the regiment is organized the same. It is comprised of a headquarters and headquarters company, three rifle

Above: **Rangers from the 1st Ranger Battalion receive Bronze Stars and Army Commendation Medals for their actions in Iraq and Afghanistan. The ceremony took place at Hunter Army Airfield on January 15, 2004.**

Left: **On January 15, 2004, Staff Sergeant Joshua Marple, squad leader in C Company, 1st Ranger Battalion, received the Bronze Star for his actions performed while rescuing Private First Class Jessica Lynch from enemy captors in Iraq.**

Rangers unload from an M2 Bradley fighting vehicle after rehearsing for a mission in support of Operation Iraqi Freedom (OIF) in Iraq. The harsh desert environment requires tough vehicles that can withstand the elements. SOCOM

platoons, and a weapons platoon. The weapons platoon of each rifle company contains a mortar section of two 60mm mortars with a third available for special operations and an antitank section of three two-man teams firing the 84mm Carl Gustav antiarmor weapon system.

The weapons platoon also encompasses the highly and specifically trained ranger sniper team. This two-man team can engage targets at 1,000 meters with pinpoint and deadly accuracy. Presently, each sniper team is issued the Barrett M82A1 semiautomatic .50-caliber sniper rifle. During the Civil War, Hiram Berdan of the Union forces and Robert E. Lee of the Confederates were the first in history to set up units of designated sharpshooters. The first U.S. Army Sniper School was set up in 1954–1955 during the Korean War by the AMU (Army Marksmanship Unit). The current U.S. Army Sniper School was established in 1987.

The army maintains the regiment at a high level of readiness. Each battalion can deploy anywhere in the world with 18 hours notice. Because of the importance the army places on the 75th Ranger Regiment, it must possess a number of capabilities. These capabilities include:

- Infiltrating and exfiltrating by land, sea, and air
- Conducting direct-action operations
- Conducting raids
- Recovery of personnel and special equipment
- Conducting conventional or special light-infantry operations

Rangers are usually limited to operations three days in length (or less), because these short missions wouldn't require resupply. A typical ranger mission might require seizing an airfield for use by the general-purpose forces that are already in transport and conducting raids on key operational and strategic targets in order to better secure the area. Once the follow-up forces arrive, the Rangers move out.

To maintain readiness, Rangers train constantly. Their training encompasses arctic, jungle, desert, and mountain operations, as well as amphibious instruction. The unit's high state of readiness dictates the training philosophy of the 75th Ranger Regiment. The philosophy includes performance-oriented training emphasizing tough standards and a focus on realism and live-fire exercises, while concentrating on the basics and safety. Training events held at night, during adverse weather, or on difficult terrain multiplies their benefits. Throughout training, Rangers are taught to expect the unexpected. As a special forces unit, the 75th Ranger Regiment believes in and operates on these truths: *humans* are more important than *hardware*, *quality* is better than *quantity*, special operations forces cannot be mass produced, and competent special operations forces cannot be created after emergencies occur. Training reinforces these truths.

All officers and enlisted soldiers in the regiment are four-time volunteers—for the army, the airborne school, the ranger regiment, and the Ranger School. Those volunteers selected for the 75th Ranger Regiment must meet tough physical, mental, and moral criteria. All commissioned officers and combat-arms noncommissioned officers (NCO) must be airborne and ranger qualified and have demonstrated a proficiency in the duty position that they are seeking.

Upon selection and assignment to the regiment, both officers and senior noncommissioned officers attend the ranger orientation program (ROP) to integrate them into the regiment. The ROP familiarizes them with regimental policies, standing operating procedures, the commander's intent, and ranger standards. Enlisted soldiers assigned to the regiment go through the ranger indoctrination program (RIP). The RIP assesses rangers' physical qualifications and indoctrinates them with basic regimental standards. Soldiers must pass ROP or RIP to be assigned to the 75th Ranger Regiment.

Junior enlisted soldiers who are not ranger qualified must attend a pre-ranger course, which ensures they are administratively, physically, and mentally prepared before they attend the U.S. Army ranger course. The result of this demanding selection and training process is a Ranger who can lead effectively against enormous mental and physical odds.

The mission of Ranger School is to conduct ranger and long-range-surveillance leader courses to further develop the combat-arms skills of officers and enlisted volunteers who are eligible for assignment to units whose primary mission is to engage in close-combat direct-fire battle. The Ranger School program is not designed to be a leadership course; any leadership skills that are learned are a secondary benefit.

Troop-leading procedures are the steps a leader undergoes in preparing his unit to accomplish a tactical combat mission. This process may be studied in books,

Prior to a mission, Rangers check their weapons and ammunition. They review the plan and know their options. Every man knows all aspects of the mission, so if key leaders are killed or wounded, other Rangers can carry on and complete the mission.

but it is the practical implementation of planning each and every detail that truly trains a leader to prepare the men and resources. In a ranger battalion, Rangers learn from each other through the do-as-I-do method. Enlisted Rangers learn many of the troop-leading procedures by being the recipients of the mission. Leaders are placed where they can best control formations. This allows the fire-team leader to lead by example: "Follow me, and do as I do."

Ranger missions are supported by a number of other special operations forces units. Here, a Task Force 160 AH-6 Little Bird pilot readies for a training mission at Fort Bragg, North Carolina, while supporting the 2nd Ranger Battalion. Like the Rangers, Task Force 160 pilots are on call on a rotating basis, ready to deploy within hours of notice.

The Ranger School's philosophy encompasses the possibility of human potential in relation to the level of human effort exerted. Ranger instructors realize that the individual comfort zone for effort is less than 25 percent of total human potential. Ranger School students self-impose enough effort to reach 50 percent of total human potential. The Ranger School course imposes a stress level that stretches the student to 75 percent of their potential. Reaching the maximum of 100 percent human potential would mean total exertion, or death. Ranger School instructors are well trained and very experienced in evaluating the level of each student's potential, stress threshold, and exerted effort. Since the ranger course's inception in 1951, ranger instructors have trained over 35,000 students from the U.S. armed forces and military personnel from some 60 allied countries.

The 75th Ranger Regiment has a victorious heritage of unwavering pride and commendable valor. Many believe that the history of the United States Ranger began in the 1750s with Robert Rogers. The earliest organized ranger unit using ranger-type tactics was activated in 1670 to combat a hostile Wampanoag tribe under the leadership of chief Metocomet, also called King Phillip, in south-eastern Massachusetts. The Wampanoag Indians comfortably navigated the harsh lands for great distances on foot and employed concealment, long-range scouting, and swift, savage raids against their opponents, inflicting a devastating toll on colonists and their property. Standard European tactics were no match for this combination of rugged terrain and skilled enemy. Small groups of Captain Benjamin Church's men sent scouts from the settlements into the surrounding terri-tory to observe signs of the enemy and provide early warning of approaching Indian raiding parties. These scout groups sent back reports, such as, "This day, ranged 9 miles." Thus, the Ranger was born. Under the command of Captain Church, the Rangers adopted the Indian's tactics by using reconnaissance proce-dures, and then swiftly moved on foot or horseback to raid the Indian positions. Successful from the start, they expanded their overland raids to the water as well. The Rangers crushed the Indian attacks, ended King Phillip's War in 1675 and ended King Phillip's life in 1676.

During the French and Indian War (1754–1763), soldier Robert Rogers developed the warrior concept to an extent never known before. Operating in the days when

Supreme Sacrifice

Rangers who paid the supreme sacrifice during the global war on terrorism:

Soldier	Battalion	Operation	Date Killed in Action
Specialist John J. Edmunds	3rd Battalion/75th Ranger Regiment (3/75)	Operation Enduring Freedom (OEF)	October 19, 2001
Specialist Kristofor T. Stonesfier	3/75	OEF	October 19, 2001
Specialist Marc A. Anderson	1st Battalion/75th Ranger Regiment (1/75)	OEF	March 4, 2002
Corporal Matthew A. Commons	1/75	OEF	March 4, 2002
Sergeant Bradley S. Crose	1/75	OEF	March 4, 2002
Staff Sergeant Nino D. Livaudais	3/75	Operation Iraqi Freedom (OIF)	April 3, 2003
Specialist Ryan P. Long	3/75	OIF	April 3, 2003
Captain Russell B. Rippetoe	3/75	OIF	April 3, 2003
Corporal Andrew F. Chris	3/75	OIF	June 26, 2003
Sergeant Timothy M. Conneway	3/75	OIF	June 28, 2003
Sergeant Jay A. Blessing	2nd Battalion/75th Ranger Regiment	OEF	November 14, 2003
Specialist Patrick D. Tillman	2/75	OEF	April 22, 2004
Private First Class Nathan E. Stahl	2/75	OIF	September 21, 2004
Corporal William M. Amundson	3/75	OEF	October 18, 2004

Rangers Killed in Action

Grenada

Sergeant Randy E. Cline
A Company, 1st Battalion (Ranger), 75th Infantry
Killed in action October 25, 1983

Sergeant Phillip S. Grenier
A Company, 2nd Battalion (Ranger), 75th Infantry
Killed in action October 25, 1983

Sergeant Kevin J. Lannon
A Company, 2nd Battalion (Ranger), 75th Infantry
Killed in action October 25, 1983

Private First Class Markin R. Maynard
A Company, 1st Battalion (Ranger), 75th Infantry
Killed in action October 25, 1983

Sergeant Mark A. Rademacher
A Company, 1st Battalion (Ranger), 75th Infantry
Killed in action October 25, 1983

Private First Class Russell L. Robinson
A Company, 1st Battalion (Ranger), 75th Infantry
Killed in action October 25, 1983

Sergeant Stephen E. Slater
A Company, 2nd Battalion (Ranger), 75th Infantry
Killed in action October 25, 1983

Specialist Four Mark O. Yamane
A Company, 1st Battalion (Ranger), 75th Infantry
Killed in action October 25, 1983

Republic of Panama

Staff Sergeant Larry Barnard
B Company, 3rd Battalion, 75th Ranger Regiment
Killed in action December 20, 1989

Private First Class Roy Brown Jr.
A Company, 3rd Battalion, 75th Ranger Regiment
Killed in action December 20, 1989

Specialist Philip Lear
B Company, 2nd Battalion, 75th Ranger Regiment
Killed in action December 20, 1989

Private First Class James W. Markwell
C Company, 1st Battalion, 75th Ranger Regiment
Killed in action December 20, 1989

Private First Class John Mark Price
A Company, 2nd Battalion, 75th Ranger Regiment
Killed in action December 20, 1989

Somalia

Corporal James M. Cavaco
B Company, 3rd Battalion, 75th Ranger Regiment
Killed in action October 3, 1993

Sergeant James C. Joyce
B Company, 3rd Battalion, 75th Ranger Regiment
Killed in action October 3, 1993

Specialist Richard W. Kowalewski
B Company, 3rd Battalion, 75th Ranger Regiment
Killed in action October 3, 1993

Sergeant Dominick M. Pilla
B Company, 3rd Battalion, 75th Ranger Regiment
Killed in action October 3, 1993

Sergeant Lorenzo M. Ruiz
B Company, 3rd Battalion, 75th Ranger Regiment
Killed in action October 3, 1993

Corporal James E. Smith
B Company, 3rd Battalion, 75th Ranger Regiment
Killed in action October 3, 1993

Up and over the top! A Ranger from 1st Battalion heads out of a berm and runs 150 yards to the first building on an objective. The building was hit with M224 60mm mortars and AH-6 Little Bird's 2.7mm rockets prior to the Rangers ever setting foot on the objective.

Charged with electric energy, this Ranger moves forward to the objective. Rangers train to fight harder and move faster. Their training teaches them to expect the unexpected and be prepared for all possibilities.

Rangers on this raid move from the safety of a covered position to new positions under the protection of covering fire from the support berm a few hundred meters away. M240s and M2 .50-caliber machine guns pound the objective as men move to take out and clear the first few buildings on the training exercise.

A Ranger School student stands in front of a ranger instructor (RI) after being "smoked" for arriving too late for formation. Rangers in the 75th Ranger Regiment will go to Ranger School within 6 to 12 months of assignment to a ranger battalion as long as they demonstrate the motivation, skills, and dedication to succeed and graduate.

commanders personally recruited their men, he was articulate and persuasive and knew his trade. Rogers had a magnetic personality and recruited nine companies of American colonists to fight for the British during the French and Indian War. Rogers published a list of 28 common-sense principles, known as Standing Orders for Rogers' Rangers, that stressed operational readiness, security, and tactics. (This list has since been abbreviated into 19 clear, simple statements.) He expounded upon the natural abilities of the frontiersmen by organizing tactics similar to guerrilla warfare. Rogers established a training program in which he personally supervised the application of his 28 standing orders. In June , 1758, Robert Rogers was conducting live-fire training exercises.

Rogers' rate of success was undeniable. His most notorious expedition was an exceptional raid against the Abenaki Indians, a fierce and violent force. With 200 Rangers moving by boat and traversing land, Rogers covered 400 miles in about 60 days. Losses were encountered en route, but the Rangers successfully penetrated deep into Indian territory. The Rangers stealthily raided and destroyed the settlement, killing several hundred enemies, thus extinguishing the threat of the Abenaki Indians.

Over the next 50 years, every conflict included American frontiersmen who formed into ranger companies led by exceptional commanders in overland and water movements, ambushes and raids, and reconnaissance patrols. On June 14, 1775, with war against the British looming dangerously close, the Continental Congress declared that six companies of expert riflemen immediately be formed. In 1777, George Washington called this force of frontiersmen "The Corps of Rangers." Under the leadership of Colonel Daniel Morgan, these ranger companies from Pennsylvania, Virginia, and Maryland earned a reputation as the most famous corps of the Continental Army. They were not Rangers in the strictest sense, but they were superior marksmen and, according to one British general, a corps of "crack shots." Morgan's riflemen achieved an impressive victory against the British at the battle of Cowpens in 1781. Attacked by 1,100 British soldiers, Morgan's Rangers killed 110 and captured 830 with a loss of 12 soldiers killed and 63 wounded.

Morgan's Rangers was not the only successful ranger outfit of the Revolutionary War. Thomas Knowlton's Rangers from Connecticut was comprised of fewer than 150 men whose missions were primarily reconnaissance. In the southern region during the Revolutionary War, a

Excerpt from the Ranger Handbook:

Principles of Patrolling. All patrols are governed by five principles.

Planning. Quickly make a simple plan and effectively communicate it to the lowest level. A great plan that takes forever to complete and is poorly disseminated isn't a great plan. Plan and prepare to a realistic standard, and rehearse everything.

Reconnaissance. Your responsibility as a Ranger leader is to confirm what you think you know, and to find out what you don't.

Security. Preserve your force as a whole, and your recon assets in particular. Every Ranger and every rifle counts; anyone could be the difference between victory and defeat.

Control. Clear concept of the operation and commander's intent, coupled with disciplined communications, to bring every man and weapon you have available to overwhelm your enemy at the decisive point.

Common Sense. Do what you're supposed to do, without someone having to tell you, despite your own personal discomfort or fear.

Acting as a finely tuned unit, Rangers cover each other's movements and anticipate the next course of action for each member. Urban operations pose unexpected outcomes around each corner. Leaving the objective after clearing rooms in a building near an airfield, Rangers support one another with MK48 and M240 machine guns along with other crew-served weapons.

ranger element was organized by the infamous Francis Marion, also known as "Swamp Fox." Operating out of the South Carolina swamps, Marion's men, numbering several hundred, disrupted British communications and supply trains and captured enemy troops. In most cases, Marion's strategy involved hitting the British forces hard and fast, rapidly destroying their forces and supplies, then fading into the dense woods or murky swamps before British reinforcements could arrive. Marion and his men were chased by English forces several times, but they were never caught. Again, tactics of guerrilla-like warfare were successfully used.

During the War of 1812, Congress called for the formation of new ranger units to serve on the western frontier and protect border towns against attacks by American Indians. The December 28, 1813, issue of the *Army Register* lists officers for 12 companies of Rangers. In the 1830s, the Texas Rangers were established along the Texas border.

Other than these accounts, there was very little in terms of official ranger units until the Civil War.

During the Civil War, many Confederate ranger units were formed, although very few operated as true ranger units and instead took the ranger name, wreaking havoc on any enemy who crossed their path. By February of 1864, few ranger units were left in the Confederate Army, but those that remained were expertly effective. Perhaps the best known Rangers of the Civil War period were commanded by Confederate Colonel John S. Mosby. Beginning as a three-man scout unit in 1862, Mosby's force grew into eight companies of Rangers by 1865. Mosby deployed small numbers on his raids, usually 20 to 50 men. His Rangers successfully infiltrated and operated behind Union lines. Mosby used aggressive action and surprise assaults to confuse the enemy and diffuse its strength, and scouts conducted reconnaissance to locate the weakest links in the

Major Robert Rogers' Rules of Discipline

[Original spelling maintained]

These volunteers I formed into a company by themselves, and took the more immediate command and management of them to myself; and for their benefit and instruction reduced into writing the following rules or plan or discipline, which, on various occasions, I had found by experience to be necessary and advantageous.

All Rangers are to be subject to the rules and articles of war; to appear at roll call every evening, on their own parade, equipped, each with a firelock, sixty rounds of powder and ball, and a hatchet, at which time an officer from each company is to inspect the same, to see they are in order, so as to be ready on any emergency to march at a minute's warning; and before they are dismissed, the necessary guards are to be draughted and scouts for the next day appointed.

Whenever you are ordered out to the enemies' forts or frontiers for discoveries, if your number be small, march in a single file, keeping at such distance from each other as to prevent one shot from killing two men, sending one man, or more, forward, and the like on each side, at the distance of twenty yards from the main body, if the ground you march over will admit of it, to give the signal to the officer of the approach of an enemy, and of their number &c.

If you march over marshes or soft ground, change your position, and march abreast of each other to prevent the enemy from tracking you (as they would do if you marched in a single file) till you get over such ground, and then resume your former order and march till it is quite dark before you encamp, which do, if possible, on a piece of ground which that may afford your centries the advantage of seeing or hearing the enemy some considerable distance, keeping one half of your whole party awake alternately through the night.

Some time before you come to the place you would reconnoitre make a stand, and send one or two men in whom you can confide, to look out the best ground for making your observations.

If you have the good fortune to take any prisoners, keep them separate, till they are examined, and in your return take a different route from that in which you went out, that you may the better discover any party in your rear, and have an opportunity, if their strength be superior to yours, to alter your course, or disperse, as circumstances may require.

If you march in a large body of three or four hundred, with a design to attack the enemy, divide your party into three columns, each headed by a proper officer, and let those columns march in single files, the columns to the right and left keeping at twenty yards distance or more from that of the center, if the ground will admit, and let proper guards be kept in the front and rear, and suitable flanking parties at a due distance as before directed, with orders to halt on all eminences, to take a view of the surrounding ground, to prevent your being ambuscaded, and to notify the approach or retreat of the enemy, that proper dispositions may be made for attacking, defending, &c. And if the enemy approach in your front on level ground, form a front of your three columns or main body with the advanced guard, keeping out your flanking parties, as if you were marching under the command of trusty officers, to prevent the enemy from pressing hard on either of your wings, or surrounding you, which is the usual method of the savages, if their number will admit of it, and be careful likewise to support and strengthen your rear guard.

If you are obliged to receive the enemy's fire, fall, or squat down, till it is over; then rise and discharge at them. If their main body is equal to yours, extend yourselves occasionally; but if superior, be careful to support and strengthen your flanking parties, to make them equal to theirs, that if possible you may repulse them to their main body, in which case push upon them with the greatest resolution with equal force in each flank and in the center, observing to keep at a due distance from each other, and advance from tree to tree, with one half of the party before the other ten or twelve yards. If the enemy push upon you, let your front fire and fall down, and then let your rear advance thro' them and do the like, by which time those who before were in front will be ready to discharge again, and repeat the same alternatively, as occasion shall require; by this means you will keep up such a constant fire, that the enemy will not be able easily to break your order, or gain your ground.

If you oblige the enemy to retreat, be careful, in your pursuit of them to keep out your flanking parties, and prevent them from gaining eminences, or rising grounds, in which case they would perhaps be able to rally and repulse you in their turn.

If you are obliged to retreat, let the front of your whole party fire and fall back, till the rear hath done the same, making for the best ground you can; by this means you will oblige the enemy to pursue you, if they do it at all, in the face of a constant fire.

If the enemy is so superior that you are in danger of being surrounded by them, let the whole body disperse, and every one take a different road to the place of rendezvous appointed for that evening, which must every morning be altered and fixed for the evening ensuing, in order to bring the whole party, or as many of them as possible, together, after any separation that may happen in the day; but if you should happen to be actually surrounded, form yourselves into a square, or if in the woods, a circle is best, and, if possible, make a stand till the darkness of the night favours your escape.

If your rear is attacked, the main body and flankers must face about to the right or left, as occasion shall require, and form themselves to oppose the enemy, as before directed; and the same method must be observed, if attacked in either of your flanks, by which means you will always make a rear of one of your flank guards.

If you determine to rally after a retreat, in order to make a fresh stand against the enemy, by all means endeavour to do it on the most rising ground you come at, which will give you greatly the advantage in point of situation, and enable you to repulse superior numbers.

In general, when pushed upon by the enemy, reserve your fire till they approach very near, which will then put them into the greatest surprize and consternation, and give you an opportunity of rushing upon them with your hatchets and cutlasses to the better advantage.

When you encamp at night, fix your centries in such a manner as not to be relieved from the main body till morning, profound secrecy and silence being often of the last importance in these cases. Each centry therefore should consist of six men, two of whom must be constantly alert, and when relieved by their fellows, it should be done without noise; and in case those on duty see or hear any thing, which alarms them, they are not to speak, but one of them is silently to retreat, that proper dispositions may be made; and all occasional centries should be fixed in like manner.

At the first dawn of day, awake your whole detachment; that being the time when the savages chuse to fall upon their enemies, you should by all means be in readiness to receive them.

If the enemy should be discovered by your detachments in the morning, and their numbers are superior to yours, and a victory doubtful, you should not attack them till the evening, as then they will not know your numbers, and if you are repulsed, your retreat will be favoured by the darkness of the night.

Before you leave your encampment, send out small parties to scout round it, to see if there be any appearance or track of an enemy that might have been near you during the night.

When you stop for refreshment, chuse some spring or rivulet if you can, and dispose your party so as not to be surprised, posting proper guards and centries at a due distance, and let a small party waylay the path came in, lest the enemy should be pursuing.

If, in your return, you have to cross rivers, avoid the usual fords as much as possible, lest the enemy should have discovered, and be there expecting you.

If you have to pass by lakes, keep at some distance from the edge of the water, lest, in case of an ambuscade or an attack from the enemy, when in that situation, your retreat should be cut off.

If the enemy pursue your rear, take a circle till you come to your own tracks, and there form an ambush to receive them, and give them the first fire.

When you return from a scout, and come near our forts, avoid the usual roads, and avenues thereto, lest the enemy should have headed you, and lay in ambush to receive you, when almost exhausted with fatigues.

When you pursue any party that has been near our forts or encampments, follow not directly in their tracks, lest they should be discovered by their rear guards, who, at such a time, would be most alert; but endeavour, by a different route, to head and meet them in some narrow pass, or lay in ambush to receive them when and where they least expect it.

If you are to embark in canoes, battoes, or otherwise, by water, chuse the evening for the time of your embarkation, as you will then have the whole night before you, to pass undiscovered by any parties of the enemy, on hills, or other places, which command a prospect of the lake or river you are upon.

In padling or rowing, give orders that the boat or canoe next the sternmost, wait for her, and the third for the second, and the fourth for the third, and so on, to prevent separation, and that you may be ready to assist each other on any emergency.

Appoint one man in each boat to look out for fires, on the adjacent shores, from the number and size of which you may form some judgment of the number that kindled them, and whether you are able to attack them or not.

If you find the enemy encamped near the banks of a river or lake, which you imagine they will attempt to cross for their security upon being attacked, leave a detachment of your party on the opposite shore to receive them, while, with the remainder, you surprize them, having them between you and the lake or river.

If you cannot satisfy yourself as to the enemy's number and strength, from their fires, &c. conceal your boats at some distance, and ascertain their number by a reconnoitering party, when they embark, or march, in the morning, marking the course they steer, &c. when you may pursue, ambush, and attack them, or let them pass, as prudence shall direct you. In general, however, that you may not be discovered by the enemy upon the lakes and rivers at a great distance, it is safest to lay by, with your boats and party concealed all day, without noise or shew; and to pursue your intended route by night; and whether you go by land or water, give out parole and countersigns, in order to know one another in the dark, and likewise appoint a station for every man to repair to, in case of any accident that may separate you.

enemy's defense. Mosby's Rangers then attacked and achieved victory.

Equally skillful were the Rangers under the command of Colonel Turner Ashby. Ashby's Rangers served the Confederacy well as they scouted and raided large numbers of Union troops. Confederate General John Hunt Morgan and his cavalry unit formed in December, 1861, and moved deep into Union territory, wreaking total fear and chaos, causing widespread hysteria, and diverting federal soldiers from the approaching Battle of Chickamauga. General Morgan and his Rangers were finally forced to surrender near East Liverpool, Ohio.

Ranger units were part of the Union troop forces as well. Mean's Rangers succeeded in engaging and capturing a portion of Colonel Mosby's force, but never quite accomplished their original mission of eliminating Mosby's Rangers. Mean's Rangers did their fair share of capturing troops and seizing supply trains, raiding homesteads and cities, and disrupting communication routes. After the close of the Civil War, recognized army ranger units would disappear for more than 70 years.

The name "Ranger" was selected by Major General Lucian K. Truscott, United States liaison with the British general staff during World War II. Truscott submitted proposals to General George Marshall that "we undertake immediately an American unit along the lines of the British Commandos." Truscott reasoned that the "name Commandos rightfully belonged to the British, and we sought a name more typically American."

On June 19, 1942, the 1st Ranger Battalion was activated in Carrickfergus, Ireland. The ranger battalion was formed by volunteers drawn from American army units based in Northern Ireland. Then-Major William Orlando Darby was appointed as the first commander of 1st Ranger Battalion. He organized, trained, and led carefully selected men to conduct key World War II missions in North Africa, Tunisia, and Italy, to name a few. His record of success astounded military leaders, who bestowed upon him the task of training two additional ranger battalions, the 3rd and 4th. His active participation in these units led to the 1st, 3rd, and 4th Ranger Battalions to become known as Darby's Rangers.

The 2nd Ranger Battalion, activated on April 1, 1943, was trained and led by Lieutenant Colonel James Earl Rudder, who successfully carried out the most dangerous mission of the entire Omaha Beach landings in Normandy, France. On June 6, 1944, three companies of the 2nd Ranger Battalion assaulted the perpendicular cliffs of Point Du Hoc under intense gunfire and destroyed a large gun battery that would have wreaked havoc on the Allied fleets offshore. For two days and nights they fought without relief.

More time in the open means more time the enemy can fix on your drop zone, find you, and engage you as a target. Ranger missions are typically conducted during hours of limited visibility. Night covers their movements, and Rangers own the night.

During the initial assault on Omaha Beach, Brigadier General Norman D. Cota, assistant division commander of the 29th Infantry Division, realized that the invasion force must push on past the beach or suffer intolerable losses. He chose the Rangers of the 5th Battalion, led by Lieutenant Colonel Max Schneider, to make a way through the murderous fire with the command, "Rangers, lead the way off this beach!" General Cota's order has become the familiar motto, "Rangers lead the way."

Though not called Rangers, the servicemen in the 5307th Composite Unit (Provisional) carried out ranger-type missions in northern Burma from February to August, 1944. The unit's commander, Major General Frank D. Merrill, led the 5307th, which became known as Merrill's Marauders for their stamina, perseverance, and professionalism. During a campaign in Southeast Asia in

1944, Major General Merrill and his marauders distinguished themselves by climbing mountains, crossing rivers, and maneuvering through jungles to surprise the enemy. These men fought sickness and exhaustion, as well as the Japanese. The group was disbanded after three months of fighting and losing 80 percent of its 3,000 volunteers to disease and combat. Merrill's Marauders ended their successful seizure of Myitkyina Airfield in north Burma and are considered true Rangers by today's veteran groups.

The 6th Battalion was formed in September, 1944, in the Pacific theater, and its commanding officer was Lieutenant Colonel Henry Mace. The 6th Ranger Battalion was the only one to conduct special operations during World War II. In January, 1945, the 6th Ranger Battalion returned to the Philippines and conducted a mission to rescue American and Allied prisoners of war. The Rangers made a 29-mile forced march past enemy lines in search of the Japanese prison camp at Cabanatuan, Philippines. They located the camp, crawled almost a mile over flat exposed terrain, attacked Japanese positions, and rescued more than 500 prisoners of war.

When World War II ended, the ranger units were disbanded, just as they had been after each of America's previous conflicts. Inactivated in 1945 and reactivated in 1950, Rangers continued to distinguish themselves in combat during the Korean War. In 1950, the army chief of staff selected Colonel John Gibson Van Houton to create a Ranger training program at Fort Benning, Georgia. The graduates of the school were organized into eight companies, each of which was attached to a conventional infantry division. They were attached first to one regiment, then to another. They performed scouting, patrols, raids, and ambushes, spearheaded assaults, and served as counterattack forces to restore lost positions. The Rangers were again inactivated in 1951.

Years later, smaller ranger units were formed in the Vietnam War, although these units were formed primarily to conduct long-range surveillance. In Vietnam, the long-range reconnaissance patrols (LRRPs) would inherit the ranger lineage. Thirteen LRRP companies were assigned to brigades, divisions, and field units to act as eyes and ears in land claimed by the Viet Cong and the North Vietnamese army. They would work in small groups, and LRRP teams would attack the enemy using hit-and-run raids and ambushes. The LRRPs were disbanded at the end of the Vietnam War, and the unit was eventually redesignated the 75th Infantry Regiment (Ranger) on June 1, 1969.

In 1973, General Creighton Abrams, army chief of staff, authorized a battalion-sized ranger unit. General Abrams offered this declaration in the *Abrams Charter* of 1973: "The ranger battalion is to be an elite, light, and most proficient infantry battalion in the world; a battalion that can do things with its hands and weapons better than anyone. The battalion will not contain any 'hoodlums' or 'brigands' and if the battalion is formed of such persons, it will be disbanded. Wherever the battalion goes, it will be apparent that it is the best." On January 28, 1974, the 1st Battalion, 75th Ranger Regiment, was activated at Fort Benning, Georgia. On July 1, 1974, the 1st Battalion, 75th Ranger Regiment, moved to Fort Stewart (Hunter Army Airfield), Georgia. On October 1, 1974, the 2nd Battalion, 75th Ranger Regiment, was activated at Fort Lewis, Washington. The ranger force grew to over 2,000 by 1984.

The 1st Battalion, 75th Infantry (Ranger), participated in a Desert One mission, Operation Eagleclaw, the 1980 Iranian hostage rescue attempts. The Rangers were to fly from Egypt to a city 35 miles south of Teheran and secure the airfield there. Once the airfield was secured, the Rangers would maintain control for however long was necessary as C-141s arrived to airlift the hostages and their rescuers back to Egypt. Desert One was aborted at the first stage when two Sea Stallions crashed into each other on landing, killing the crews.

On October 25, 1983, at 0534, the first Rangers began low-level parachute assault from 500 feet at Point Salines on the island of Grenada. The 1st Ranger Battalion began the assault and was followed by the 2nd Battalion, and later, the 82nd Airborne forces. The operation's mission was to protect the lives of American citizens and restore democracy to the island. Code-named Urgent Fury, the Rangers secured the airfield and the True Blue Campus at Point Salines, where American medical students were in residence. The Rangers also conducted air assault operations to eliminate pockets of resistance and seized control of the Richmond Hill prison and army camp at Calivigny.

On October 3, 1984, the Department of the Army activated the 3rd Ranger Battalion, and on February 3, 1986, the 75th Ranger Regimental Headquarters Company was activated; both are stationed at Fort Benning, Georgia. This marked a new era for the Rangers. With over 2,000 soldiers, the three battalions and regimental headquarters had a force of men not seen since World War II.

The entire ranger regiment participated in Operation Just Cause, the invasion of Panama on December 20, 1989, which restored democracy to the Central American country. Conducting simultaneous low-level parachute jumps, the Rangers secured Torrijos-Tocumen International Airport, Rio Hato Military Airfield, and General Manuel Noriega's beach house. They secured airfields for the arrival of the 82nd Airborne Division, and Rangers moved into Panama City and took the military headquarters of the Panamanian Defense Force. The Rangers accomplished their mission and removed Manuel Noriega, his loyalists, and members of the Panamanian Defense Force from power. After capturing 1,014 enemy prisoners of war and over 18,000 arms of various types and sustaining five killed and 42 wounded, the Rangers returned home on January 7, 1990.

The Rangers fought again in Operation Desert Storm, in which elements of B Company, 1st Battalion, 75th Ranger Regiment, and 1st Platoon with weapons platoon attachments of A Company, 1st Battalion, 75th Ranger

Regiment, deployed to Saudi Arabia from February 12, 1991, to April 15, 1991. The Rangers conducted raids and provided a quick-reaction force in cooperation with Allied forces. There were no ranger casualties. In December, 1991, 1st Battalion and the Regimental Headquarters Company deployed to Kuwait in a routine training exercise as a show of force. The Rangers jumped into Kuwait during daylight hours.

The next deployment of the Rangers occurred in Somalia in 1993 as Operation Restore Hope. The 3rd Ranger Battalion's B Company was deployed from August 26, 1993, to October 21, 1993, to assist the United Nations' forces in establishing order in a desperately corrupt and chaotic nation. A Company of the 3rd Ranger Battalion deployed to Somalia from October 5, 1993, to October 23, 1993, in support of United Nations' operations. Engaged in a civil war since 1977, where violent Somali clansmen commonly conducted killings and beheadings, the Somali government collapsed in 1991. The Rangers took part in seven missions that tried to capture Somali National Alliance (SNA) clan leader Mohammed Aidid and his top lieutenants. The nation of Somalia was starving, and Aidid's guerrilla war against the United Nations' efforts to feed the Somali people needed to end.

On October 3, 1993, B Company and members of Special Force Operational Detachment Delta, a combined group named Task Force Ranger (TFR), conducted a daylight raid in one of the most dangerous parts of Mogadishu to capture two of Aidid's officers in the Olympic Hotel. The team was successful in capturing these two officers, plus approximately 21 others, and began the extraction process within 20 minutes of the assault's commencement. Humvees were dispatched for the extraction and reached the Olympic Hotel despite an ambush by clansmen of Aidid. Two UH-60 Black Hawk helicopters were shot down by rocket-propelled grenade (RPG) rounds, and the Rangers embarked upon a courageous rescue operation that would grow into a fierce and intense firefight. The Rangers secured the downed helicopter, and another Black Hawk was shot down by RPG fire. They were pinned down by intense fire from machine guns, hand grenades, and RPGs as darkness fell, and the Rangers established a perimeter inside the nearby buildings to treat their wounded and wait for extraction. For nearly 18 hours, the Rangers stood their ground and delivered devastating firepower, killing an estimated 300 to 600 Somalis. The relief force encountered heavy fire en route to their fellow Rangers and were later reinforced with elements of the 10th Mountain Division and Pakistani and Malaysian armored vehicles that helped extract the wounded and fallen Rangers. Six Rangers were killed in action and numerous others were wounded.

The 1st Ranger Battalion was called to action in 2002 for Operation Anaconda, a mission to secure a 10,000-foot snow-capped mountain named Takur Ghar in eastern Afghanistan as an observation post for the nearby valleys. The al Qaeda enemy had a well-concealed, fortified stronghold within the crooks, crannies, and shadows of the Shahikot mountains with precisely positioned artillery to shoot down aircraft flying in the valley below. On March 4, 2002, Rangers implemented Task Force Mountain against the al Qaeda terrorists. Communications problems were terrain-driven and hampered line-of-sight communication during the seizure. The intense 17-hour firefight on top of a frigid, rugged mountain ridge with sheer drop-offs ended with the Rangers and accompanying forces securing the mountaintop and resulted in the deaths of approximately 450 Taliban and al Qaeda soldiers defending the mountain and the deaths of three Rangers of the 1st Battalion.

Deployments for the 75th Ranger Regiment are ongoing, since their expert skill, lightning speed, and commitment to duty are needed to fight the global war on terrorism in Iraq and Afghanistan, among other locations. The 75th Ranger Regiment is conducting classified missions during Operation Enduring Freedom (OEF) and Operation Iraqi Freedom (OIF). These unpublicized operations include seizures and raids. Due to observation of operational security related to tactics, techniques, and procedures, it may be years before official documents are released to tell the Rangers' stories of Iraq and Afghanistan. Rangers seized a communications outpost in Iraq near the Jordanian border. They have bravely seized airfields in western Iraq and raided enemy strongholds. They retained control of the Hadithah Dam on the Euphrates River, keeping Saddam Hussein's men from destroying it. The 1st Battalion Rangers and special operations forces participated in the successful raid to free U.S. Army POW Private Jessica Lynch.

The Rangers have led the way in battle and conflict from the beginning of our nation to the twenty-first century global war on terrorism. The courageous actions of these valiant warriors have been witnessed against overwhelming odds, chaotic mobs, corrupt clansmen, and powerful terrorists. The men of the 75th Ranger Regiment have traveled, and will continue to travel, the world over to complete their missions with pride, integrity, and quiet professionalism.

The squad leader prepares to conduct an after action review (AAR) of a training mission in a military operations in urban terrain (MOUT) environment. During the AAR, each Ranger will discuss their actions on the objective, what went as planned, and what could be improved upon. Drawings often accompany the discussions. This process helps younger Rangers learn every man's job and correct mistakes.

The Rangers'
Individual Weapons

The ranger squad arrives on the landing zone by MH-60 Black Hawk helicopter. The crew-served (meaning that it takes a two-man team to operate it effectively, the gunner and the assistant gunner) M48 gunners are the first to exit and establish a defensive position to maintain security while the remaining men depart the aircraft. Rangers spill forth from the belly of the aircraft with M4 carbines cocked and locked. Immediately, the patrol moves to the designated rally point, which may be a

Above: **The 75th Ranger Regiment has been busy fighting the global war on terrorism since 9/11, as illustrated by the two gold stars on this 3rd Ranger Battalion Ranger's airborne patch, or jump wings. Each gold star represents an airborne jump into combat. The larger single star indicates that this Ranger has earned jump master training, a specialty course in the preparation and execution of airborne insertion by parachute.**

Left: **A Ranger from 1st Battalion, 75th Ranger Regiment, stands in front of a C-130 stationed at Travis Airfield in Savannah, Georgia. This Ranger is outfitted with a Colt M4 carbine 5.56mm rifle and a Beretta 9mm pistol. An AN/PVS-14 night-vision device is perched on top of his modular information communications helmet (MICH). There are pouches and pockets for ammunition and grenades on his load-bearing equipment.**

distance and direction or a specific terrain feature. Hand and arm signals are used instead of speaking. The ranger patrol accounts for its men and begins silent movement on foot to the objective to complete the mission.

The automatic rifle is a squad leader's weapon that allows rifle squads to take a light automatic weapon with them in assaults. Though the automatic rifle has changed, the role of the automatic rifleman has not since its inception in World War I. The automatic rifleman supports the infantry squad in both offense and defense.

Colt Defense, LLC, has developed various versions of the basic AR15 and M16 carbine rifles since the 1970s. In 1994, the U.S. Army adopted the Colt Model 720 selective-fire carbine as its M4 carbine, and the rifle entered service in 1997. The Colt M4 carbine is the compact version of the M16A2 rifle and replaces the M16 series rifle. The new weapon was handier and more comfortable to carry than the long M16A2 rifle. The U.S. Army's standard-issue Colt M16A2 rifle is hailed by some as the most combat-proven weapon system in the world. The M16A2 rifle fires NATO 5.56mm caliber ammunition. It is a lightweight, air-cooled, gas-operated weapon capable of semiautomatic (single shot) and fully automatic (three-round bursts) fire. Ammunition is magazine fed. When properly zeroed and operated, it has a range of 1,000 meters. The M16A2 rifle weighs approximately 8 pounds without its sling and ammunition.

Beretta M9

Primary function: Semiautomatic pistol for personal defense

Manufacturer: Beretta and Beretta USA

Length: 8.54 inches (21.69 centimeters)

Width: 1.50 inches (3.81 centimeters)

Height: 5.51 inches (14 centimeters)

Barrel length: 4.92 inches (12.5 centimeters)

Weight unloaded: 2.1 pounds

Weight fully loaded: 2.55 pounds (1.16 kilograms)

Bore diameter: 9mm (approximately 0.355 inches)

Maximum effective range: 152.5 feet (50 meters)

Magazine capacity: 15 rounds

Muzzle velocity: 1,200 feet (365 meters) per second

The M4 carbine is similar in design and functionality to the M16 family of rifles, thereby greatly simplifying training, supply, and maintenance. Compared to the M16A2 rifle, the M4 carbine is 1.3 pounds lighter, 6 5/8 inches shorter with buttstock extended, and almost 10 inches shorter with the buttstock collapsed.

The M4 carbine is used to deter adversaries by enabling individual soldiers and small units operating in close-quarters combat situations to engage targets with accurate, lethal fire. The M4 carbine is a lightweight, gas-operated, air-cooled, magazine-fed machine gun. It fires standard NATO 5.56mm ammunition. The M4 weighs 7.5 pounds when loaded, with a sling and one magazine. As a compact version of the M16A2 rifle, it features a collapsible stock, a flat-top upper receiver with integral Picatinny-type accessory rail, and a detachable handle/rear aperture site assembly. This weapon is fired from the shoulder. The selective rate of fire, through the use of a selector lever, gives the soldier the option of either automatic fire (three-round bursts) or semiautomatic fire

Rangers from the 1st Ranger Battalion conduct military operations in urban terrain (MOUT) training at Hunter Army Airfield in Savannah, Georgia. The "shoot house" is named after 1st Battalion Ranger Specialist Marc A. Anderson, who was killed in action while fighting the Taliban and al Qaeda during Operation Anaconda in Afghanistan, March 4, 2002.

Ranger training brigade trains soldiers to become more proficient Rangers. They often conduct a demonstration for VIPs and family members during Ranger School graduation at Fort Benning, Georgia. Many of the support elements for the ranger department are graduates of Ranger School, and all the "walkers" are ranger qualified.

(single shot). It is effective between 600 (area target) and 500 meters (point target).

The M4 can be fitted with the M68 red-dot sights for combat in close quarters. It has been the standard-issue sight since 1997 for small-arms weaponry. The M68 is a reflex (non-telescopic) non-magnifying sight. It uses red-dot technology with a red aiming reference (collimated dot) that is designated for the two-eyes-open method of sighting, which promotes target engagement, safety, and situational awareness. One eye looks through the sight and aligns the dot with the target, while the other eye observes information about the surrounding field of view.

Rangers constantly train. In this daylight stress-fire exercise, Rangers use their advanced combat optical gun sight (ACOG) 4x32-power scopes to aim at a target while keeping both eyes open and remaining aware of their surroundings.

Putting rounds down range and on target is continually practiced by all Rangers, who must pass tests to qualify for using the weapon system. The 3rd Battalion Rangers fire on targets at Fort Benning, Georgia. The weapon is a Colt M4A1 carbine with an M203 40mm grenade launcher mounted to the bottom. An advanced combat optical gun sight (ACOG) scope tops the weapon system.

The M68 sight performs in any light condition from full sun to total darkness and is compatible with night-vision equipment.

EOTech Inc. manufactures a holographic weapon sights (HWS) scope as an alternative to the M68's red dot technology. Reportedly, the U.S. Special Operations Command and Marine Corps purchased holographic weapon sights and shipped them to their soldiers in Iraq and Afghanistan. The scope's electro-optic sighting system applies holographic technology to small- and medium-sized weapons. The sight projects an illuminated reticle pattern directly on the target. The laser technology

M203 Grenade Launcher

Weight: 3 pounds (empty); 3.6 pounds (loaded)
Overall length: 15 inches
Barrel length: 12 inches
Ammunition type: CN/CS/OC tear gas rounds, smoke rounds, non-lethal projectiles, signal and practice rounds, and standard 40mm rounds
Effective range: Approximately 350 yards

The special operations peculiar modification (SOPMOD) M4 accessory kit.

A 3rd Ranger Battalion squad leader clears his M4 of blank rounds to use live-fire ammunition while training for redeployment to Afghanistan. This M4 is equipped with an AN/PEQ-2 infrared pointer and illuminator, along with the advanced combat optical gun sight (ACOG) 4x32-power scope.

The Colt M4A1 rifle has been in the special operations command's inventory since about 1994 and is modified with sights, tactical lights, AN/PEQ-2 infrared pointer and illuminator, and other accessories specific to the special operations peculiar modification (SOPMOD) M4 kit. This M4 has an advanced combat optical gun sight (ACOG), 4x scope, and Harris bipod legs.

projects an image onto a hardened piece of glass, just as in the heads-up displays in fighter jets and helicopters. The HWS is compatible with night-vision goggles and can be used under water. It can survive a 10-foot drop and remain functional at temperature extremes from –40 to 150 degrees Fahrenheit.

In the global war on terrorism, Rangers find themselves in harrowing urban, mountainous, and desert arenas that call for technologically advanced weaponry and sighting systems. Confined spaces, hardened targets, and night-vision limitations of urban combat necessitate the development of more advanced and specialized equipment. In the near future, fusion technology will enable advances in night-vision goggles and weapon sights. Sensor fusion technology combines image intensification, such as that found in conventional night-vision goggles, with a thermal sensor or forward-looking infrared (FLIR) into a single image. The AN/PAS 13 thermal weapon sight will have this advanced technology and capability to further the Rangers' effectiveness in the urban environment.

The M7 bayonet knife is used on the M16 series rifle and as a hand weapon. The M7's blade and hilt are very similar to the M4 bayonet of the Korean War era. The M7

The Colt M4A1 rifle is modified for the Ranger's specific needs for each mission. A Ranger from the 1st Ranger Battalion sports a modified M4A1 sniper mission-enhanced version with silencer, bipod legs, full buttstock, and special 10x scope.

entered service in 1964 along with the M16 serviceman's rifle. The M7 will fit the M16 family of rifles, including the M4 carbine. Although originally produced by Bauer Ord Company, Colt and Ontario Knife Company made many M7 bayonets for military and commercial use. The M7 has a two-lever locking mechanism that connects to a lug on the M16 barrel. The M7 1095 carbon steel blade is 6 3/4 inches long, with an overall length of 11.9 inches. The blade is 7/8 inch wide and weighs about 9.6 ounces. One edge is sharpened along the full length, while the other side of the blade has approximately 3 inches sharpened.

In 1987, the army began distributing its new bayonet, the M9, which is used on the M16 series rifle, on the M4 series carbine, as a hand weapon, as a general field and utility knife, as a wire cutter together with its scabbard, and as a saw. The M9 can saw through 2x2-inch pine boards, aircraft fuselages, or two-strand barbed wire. The knife and scabbard together form a wire cutter by slipping the scabbard stud into the hole in the knife blade.

The M145 4-powered scope, which features a lens flare dissipater on its end, is mounted on an M240B medium machine gun.

Here comes the pain. Rangers from 3rd Battalion rush from a starting point to negotiate a variety of obstacles during a stress-fire exercise at Fort Benning, Georgia. The event is timed, and the squad must finish the obstacles as a team. During the training exercises, Rangers must don all of their equipment and weapon systems to maintain endurance, speed, and skill.

Phrobis III Ltd. designed the M9 bayonet. It weighs 1.3 pounds with the scabbard, which has a sharpening stone under a rear flap and a screwdriver at the tip. The M9 bayonet's blade measures 7x1.4 inches; the bayonet is 12 inches long overall. It features lock-release levers for the left hand and right hand.

The bayonet's evolution can be traced to rural southern France in the mid-1600s. The displeased peasants had run out of powder and shot and, in desperation, rammed their long-bladed hunting knives into their muskets' muzzles, resulting in a type of spear. Even in modern warfare bursting with technology, bayonets are issued as weapons, and most armies still train with them.

Length: 11.5 inches (M6), 11.75 inches (M7), 12 inches (M9)

Entered U.S. Army Service: M6 (1957), M7 (1964), M9 (1987)

The M203 grenade launcher is a single-shot weapon designed in the early 1970s for use with the M16 series rifle. The M203 was designed and procured as the

The M240B is the medium machine gun of the 75th Ranger Regiment. Manufactured by Fabrique Nationale, it fires a 7.62mm round and weighs 24.2 pounds. An M145 4-power scope tops this weapon system.

Moving in buddy teams, Rangers progress through a smokescreen created to cover their movement. The rest of the squad provides security in the wood line and waits for the team to be in position before they move.

Responding to an enemy threat to the front, Rangers place fire onto targets during a timed stress-fire exercise at Fort Benning, Georgia, the home of the 3rd Ranger Battalion and the 75th Ranger Regimental Headquarters.

Sporting the latest fashions for war, a Ranger from 1st Battalion has new hearing protection, an M4A1 carbine with an Aimpoint Comp-M sight, and new load-carrying equipment that integrates body armor. Everything he needs is strapped to him.

replacement for the M79 grenade launcher of the Vietnam era. Designed and manufactured by Colt, it delivers a 40mm grenade. The M203A1 is a single-shot 40mm grenade launcher designed specifically for use with the M4 carbine series. As it is used in conjunction with the M4, its use in ranger units is complementary to the individual small-arms weapon: to engage appropriate targets with powerful and lethal grenade fire. It is a lightweight, compact, breech-loading pump-action launcher. The launcher has a leaf sight and a quadrant sight. This grenade launcher is capable of firing a variety of low-velocity 40mm grenade ammunition, and the M203 is also used as the delivery system for smoke and tear gas rounds, non-lethal projectiles, and signal grenades.

Modifications to the M4 carbine have been developed as well. When compared to the M4, the M4A1 boasts a modified trigger unit to fire as a fully automatic weapon rather than the M4's three-round bursts. The M4A1 special operations peculiar modification (SOPMOD) kit was developed

Ranger School students conduct patrolling operations waist-deep in the murky swamps of southern Florida. The students will spend the next six days in the swamps conducting follow-on missions.

Ambush! Members of the 1st Ranger Battalion conduct an ambush at 0330 hours to engage enemy targets in the kill zone. Tracers and blasts from claymore mines rip though the land and leave nothing unscathed.

Armed with an M4 carbine and an M203 grenade launcher, a Ranger School student patrols the swamps of Florida. The M203 is a single-feed, breech-loading weapon with 40mm high-explosive smoke, buckshot, marking, and practice rounds.

Trijicon's advanced combat optical gun sight (ACOG) is an aiming sight that uses a 4x unit with tritium and fiber optic technology to illuminate the reticle, thus referred to as the ACOG 4x telescopic. The reticle is very quick up close, and the 4x magnification is useful at longer range. Because the advanced fiber optics collect and use surrounding ambient light, the ACOG can be used in low light or at night. Its exterior is made of forged aircraft-strength aluminum. The sight mounts to the M4 carbine's flat-top receiver and weighs only 3/4 pound.

The M4A1 special operations peculiar modification version is lightweight, flexible, and offers ideal firepower. Some reports of the latest experiences in Afghanistan, however, suggest that the M4A1 has some flaws:

- The shorter barrel commands lower bullet velocities, which significantly decrease the effective range of the 5.56mm bullet.
- The M4 barrel rapidly overheats.
- The shortened barrel results in a shortened gas system, which works under greater pressures than the M16A2 rifle. This increases the rate of fire but produces more stress on the moving parts, thus decreasing reliability.

Rangers patrol the swamps of Florida while working in platoon-size elements and conducting raids and ambushes. Decades ago, water and swamp environments were common to Ranger operations. Because of the global war on terrorism, Rangers now spend much of their time patrolling in desert mobility vehicles in the Middle East supporting Operation Iraqi Freedom (OIF)/Operation Enduring Freedom (OEF).

specifically with the Rangers in mind. It features an M4A1 carbine equipped with the rail interface system (RIS) instead of the standard hand guards. The rail interface system consists of numbered notches along the top, bottom, and both sides of the M4's barrel. This allows the gun's operator to easily attach the various components of the SOPMOD kit. The kit includes a variety of additional upgrades to the basic M4 options, such as various sights (ACOG 4x telescopic, ACOG Reflex red dot, detachable back-up open sights), laser pointers (visible and infrared), detachable sound suppressors, and a modified M203 40mm grenade launcher with shortened barrel and improved sights. The kit also included a detachable front grip and tactical light.

A Ranger noncommissioned officer gives a class on the M203 grenade launcher. The M203 can fire several different rounds, including the M433 high explosive dual-purpose (HEDP) round, M397 airburst round, M576 buckshot round, M992 infrared illumination round, M651 combat support round, M583A1 white phosphate round, M585 white star cluster, M661 green star cluster, M662 red star cluster, and M713 ground marking round.

The Trijicon advanced combat optical gun sight (ACOG) has 4x magnification and is highly durable due to its airplane-grade aluminum alloy body. Rangers wear Wiley X ballistic eye protection but will change to Oakley eye protection in the future.

By some accounts, the M4A1 is less than ideal for special operations troops. Rangers of the 1st Battalion claimed preference for the M4A1 carbine over the XM8 and cited the weapon as reliable and actively compatible with high-tech sights, launchers, close-quarter combat devices, and computer equipment. Introduction of a new weapon system that does not interface with presently available additional equipment would be detrimental to the Rangers' functionality in the field. Further development and testing is necessary to determine the XM8's practical application on the war front. The XM8 was developed by the U.S. Army's office of Project Manager for Soldier Weapons located at Picatinny Arsenal, New Jersey, in conjunction with the U.S. Army Infantry Center. The XM8 future combat rifle is under consideration to replace existing M4 carbines and select 5.56mmx45 weapons in the U.S. Army arsenal.

Still under development, the XM8 lightweight assault rifle is purported to reduce operator load, increase mobility, and meet a variety of needs on the battlefield. The XM8 is not a single weapon, but a standard weapon with three additional versions. Each version fires a

Part of the special operations peculiar modification (SOPMOD) M4 kit is the QD sound suppressor that reduces the sound of firing the weapon by 30 decibels. This M4 also has a white light, an AN/PEQ-2 infrared pointer, and an Aimpoint Comp-M sight.

magazine-fed NATO 5.56mm round of ammunition. The standard model is 6.2 pounds and under 30 inches in length. The sharpshooter version is designed for increased range, and the auto-rifle version serves as a squad automatic weapon option. A compact version is designed for close-quarters battle. Unlike its predecessors, the M16 series and the M4 carbine rifles, the XM8 rifle is powered by a gas system that does not introduce gases and carbon back into the weapon during firing, reducing mechanical failure and increasing reliability.

The Beretta M9 personal defense weapon is the primary side arm of the United States military and replaces the .45-caliber model M1911A1. The Beretta M9 is a semiautomatic double-action pistol that fires 9mm NATO round ammunition. This compact pistol weighs only 2 1/2 pounds with its fully loaded 15-round staggered magazine. The M9 has redundant automatic safety features to help prevent accidental discharges. It can be fired in double- or single-action mode and can be unloaded without activating the trigger while the safety is on. The M9 hammer can be lowered from the cocked position to the uncocked position without activating the trigger.

Members of the 3rd Ranger Battalion move in a wedge formation to the line of departure and onto the contact lane for a blank-fire exercise.

A Ranger fire team provides security on an objective during a mission in support of Operation Iraqi Freedom (OIF) in Iraq. SOCOM

After high crawling 20 yards, a Ranger from the 3rd Ranger Battalion drops to the ground and engages hard targets during a street-fire exercise. The Rangers are timed on all of these events. Both speed and accuracy, or reaction to contact, are important. Squad leaders have been training personnel new to the battalion on standard operating procedures.

The Barrett .50-caliber sniper rifle has a 9x49-power Bushnell scope and can hit targets over 1,000 meters away. The bipod legs steady this weapon. Sniper teams consist of a spotter and a shooter.

A sniper from the 1st Ranger Battalion focuses on a target through the scope of his Stone SR-25 weapon while in Afghanistan. SOCOM

Snipers from the 1st Ranger Battalion prepare for a mission. The Barrett .50-caliber sniper rifle has seen many kills in the global war on terrorism by members of the 75th Ranger Regiment.

The M9 Beretta 9mm pistol is the standard side arm of the ranger regiment. Unlike other special operations forces, Rangers do not have the luxury of substituting their side arms for other options that may possess greater power.

Rangers from the 1st Battalion disassemble the Beretta M9 9mm pistol during expert infantryman's badge (EIB) training at Hunter Army Airfield. To earn their EIB, Rangers must pass a series of infantry skill tests. All of these Rangers have been awarded their combat infantryman's badge (CIB) as a result of their participation in Operation Iraqi Freedom (OIF)/Operation Enduring Freedom (OEF).

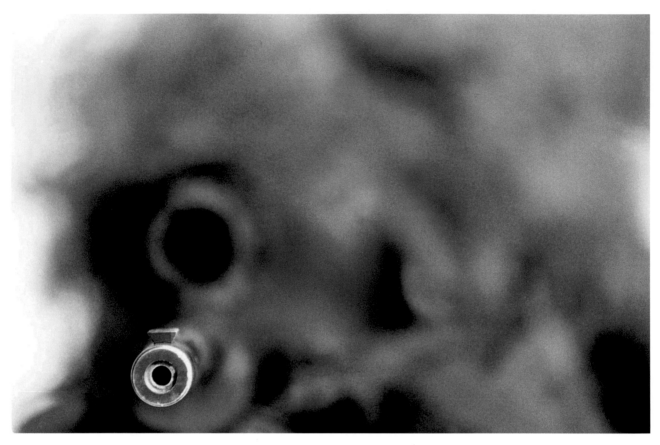

Ranger snipers are highly trained and adapt well to their environment. The ranger regiment employs a number of sniper systems, the M24, the Stoner SR-25, and the Barrett M82A1 .50-caliber rifle.

The M24 sniper rifle has a Picatinny rail interface system with a multi-notched rail for attaching a wide variety of optical sights and night-vision optics.

Ranger snipers are masters of camouflage and concealment. The ranger sniper uses his rucksack to support his M24 rifle and fire upon targets 300 meters away.

Rangers from the 3rd Ranger Battalion conduct stress-fire exercises in preparation for returning deployment to Iraq and Afghanistan. The Ranger crawls through a wire obstacle to engage hard targets at the end of the lane.

The Arsenal of Firepower

The 75th Ranger Regiment has priority in the issuance of new equipment. Portable weapons; lightweight clothing and equipment; improved rations; the latest communications equipment; and surveillance, target acquisition, and night observation (STANO) devices are supplied to ranger units as soon as they are ready for use. In response to an urgent need from U.S. Army soldiers serving in Iraq, the U.S. Army Research, Development, and Engineering Center (ARDEC) at Picatinny Arsenal, New Jersey, has released three dozen new systems and conducted in-theater training on the new equipment.

Advanced surveillance, target acquisition, and night observation (STANO) equipment is either active or passive. Active STANO equipment projects some form of energy.

Above: **The Browning M2 .50-caliber machine gun is mounted on a desert mobility vehicle (DMV) in support of Rangers moving from a concealed position. The team on the DMV disembarks from the vehicle and moves forward to begin a timed exercise.**

Left: **While training for an expert infantryman's badge (EIB), a Ranger is performing a function check on the M2 Browning .50-caliber heavy machine gun. Rangers deploy these heavy weapons on desert mobility vehicles (DMVs) and pull them on Skedco stretchers to the support berms to have a heavy volume of covering fire for the assaulting elements.**

This energy, likely radio frequency or infrared, can be detected by the enemy. Passive STANO equipment either detects existing energy emissions or uses available light as a means of detection. Use of passive equipment is usually not detectable by the enemy. Active STANO equipment is generally limited to infrared illumination devices. Objects illuminated by these active devices are viewed using passive STANO equipment. There are two categories of passive STANO equipment: image-intensification devices and thermal-imagery devices.

Standardized available resources and equipment are consistent between the ranger battalions. Firepower is essential. Each battalion is allotted these weapon systems as a standard: 84mm ranger antitank weapon systems (RAWS), 60mm mortars, MK46 special purpose weapon (SPW), MK48 lightweight machine gun, MK19 grenade launchers, M2 .50-caliber machine guns, and Javelins.

MACHINE GUNS AND AUTOMATIC WEAPONS SYSTEMS

The Browning M2 .50-caliber machine gun is an automatic, belt-fed, crew-operated weapon. Although the 128-pound gun and tripod are transportable with limited amounts of ammunition for short distances, the gun is usually not the

Men from the 2nd Ranger Battalion are in the older ranger special operations vehicle (RSOV). The mounted M2 .50-caliber machine gun would have little or no protection against small-arms fire. The RSOV has been replaced by the ground/desert mobility vehicle, a modified Humvee that is better equipped for desert and mountain terrains.

In training at Fort Campbell, Kentucky, Rangers from the 1st Battalion move other vehicles forward as this one provides covering fire. The gunner braces himself behind the M2 .50-caliber machine gun mounted to the top of a desert mobility vehicle. The vehicle's driver radios coordinates to the advancing patrol. SOCOM

choice of the highly mobile light infantry Rangers. The M2 may be mounted on ground mounts and most vehicles as antipersonnel and antiaircraft weapons. The ranger battalion more frequently mounts the M2 on its GMV as an antipersonnel or antiaircraft weapon, which yields a maximum effective range of 2,000 meters. The aviators of Task Force 160 mount this massive machine gun to their AH-6 Little Birds and the MH-53 Pave Low helicopters. The M2 provides suppressive fire for offensive and defensive purposes against light armored vehicles, low- and slow-flying aircraft, personnel, and small boats. Twelve M2 machine guns are supplied per ranger battalion.

The M2 .50-caliber flexible version is used as a ground gun on the M3 tripod mount. This version cannot be used against aircraft targets. The flexible ground version possesses a single-shot option that is not available in the mounted type. The Browning M2 .50-caliber machine gun's M48 is available in turret, fixed, and soft mount types, which can be installed on combat vehicles.

The Browning M2 .50-caliber machine gun is a World War II–era automatic machine gun. Also known as "Ma Deuce" by the soldiers, the Browning M2 was one of the most important weapons in the Great War. Introduced into United States military service in 1938, the M2 is the oldest

The Browning M2 machine gun is prepared for the mission of providing heavy volumes of fire onto an enemy target and allowing the Ranger to accomplish his mission. This M2 mounted to a desert mobility vehicle, a modified Humvee, is prepared for a blank fire as it has a blank adapter attached to the barrel.

gun still used today. FN Herstal (Belgian Fabrique Nationale) is the original producer of the Browning .50-caliber machine guns. Today, the Browning M2 is manufactured by Ramo Defense in the United States, by General Dynamics in Belgium, by FN Herstal in Belgium, and by other international companies.

Today's .50-caliber machine gun was initially designed as an aircraft-mounted weapon. In 1921, it was modified for ground troop use as the Model 1921 machine gun. Years later, in 1932, the Model 1921 was modernized and adopted under the designation of M2. Later, a heavier barrel (Model M2HB) was introduced for an increased rate of fire and increased number of rounds fired between barrel changes. Disadvantages arose as every heavy barrel replacement required a time-consuming procedure that no Ranger could accommodate. Recently, the quick-change barrel (QCB) kit

The Browning M2 .50-caliber heavy machine gun is mounted on a desert mobility vehicle's turret. This powerful weapon has a cyclic rate of fire of 200 to 300 rounds per minute. The weapon can fire armor-piercing rounds to penetrate light-skinned vehicles.

was introduced. This kit permits a quick barrel change under battle conditions in any M2HB gun.

For the ranger battalion's standards, the M2HB is a heavy machine gun. Ramo Defence introduced the M2 Lightweight machine gun, weighing in at 60 pounds, 24 pounds less than its heavy predecessor. Maintaining the Browning M2's principles and utilizing almost 75 percent of the parts from the original M2, the weapon was upgraded to include: an adjustable buffer to vary the firing rate; a patented quick-change, lightweight Stellite-lined chrome-bore barrel with flash suppressor; a Max Safe charging system; and a trigger safety switch. This gun has a back plate with spade grips, trigger, and bolt latch release. It is equipped with leaf-type rear sight and a spare barrel assembly. By repositioning some of the component parts, ammunition may be fed from either the left or the right side.

The M240G gunner fires onto moving targets from 800 meters. The M240G replaced the M60 medium machine gun and fires 7.62x51mm rounds. A typical ranger gun team consists of a gunner, an assistant gunner (AG), and an ammunition bearer.

The M240G is mounted on a ranger desert mobility vehicle, the preferred use of this weapon. This machine gun is outfitted with an AN/PEQ-2 infrared pointer and illuminator, an Elcan M145 scope, and a red-tipped blank adapter. Note the touchpad above the cylindrical charging handle that activates the AN/PEQ-2 laser identifier and illuminator pointer.

Soldiers from A Company, 1st Battalion, 75th Ranger Regiment, deployed to Fort Campbell, Kentucky, participate in live-fire training. The M240G is resting on a tripod as a gunner scans his sector of fire. SOCOM

A disintegrating metallic link belt feeds the ammunition into the weapon.

The M249 squad automatic weapon system (SAWS) is a light machine gun capable of delivering a large volume of effective fire to support infantry squad operations with accuracy similar to a rifle. Although the SAWS is primarily used as an automatic rifle, it is also used as a light machine gun. It can be fired from the shoulder, hip, underarm, or from a bipod. It is a gas-operated, disintegrating metallic-link-belt-fed weapon that fires standard NATO 5.56mm ammunition. Although a 200-round disintegrating belt is standard, it can also fire a 20- or 30-round M16 magazine. Its maximum effective range is 1,000 meters. An individual can carry this weapon, as it weighs approximately 15 pounds. A gunner's basic load of 600 rounds of linked ammunition weighs little more than 20 pounds. Nicknamed the "human meat grinder" the SAWS' cyclic rate of fire at 725 rounds per minute provides the basis of firepower for the rifle team. Each ranger battalion has 54 of these weapons. Although no longer standard

The M240G fires onto targets as the assistant gunner (AG) directs the gunner to the target. The AG gives commands in small increments of meters. Communication between the AG and the gunner is integral to engaging targets and eliminating them.

"Humpin' the hog." An M240G gunner controls the most invaluable firepower in the squad, but with that awesome firepower comes the most weight to carry. Sometimes on very long movements or road marches, the gunner may trade off the weight of the machine gun with his assistant gunner for a while. Hardcore gunners wouldn't even consider trading out the load.

An M240G machine gunner and his assistant gunner run down a road to get into a support position so the assault element will have covering fire as it moves forward onto a set of targets.

weaponry in the ranger regiment, M249s are present in various units and militias in the Middle East.

The Belgian Fabrique Nationale (also referred to as FN, FN Herstal, or FN Manufacturing) designed and manufactured the XM249 Minimi, which was standardized as the M249 squad automatic weapon system in 1982. The M249 filled the void created by the retirement of the M1918A2 Browning automatic rifle (BAR) in the 1950s. Interim automatic weapons (M14 series/M16A1 rifles) had failed as viable base-of-fire weapons in infantry units and in other units requiring high firepower. The M249 has an excellent reputation of reliability and firepower; however, more recent reports indicate malfunctions and failures of M249 weapons in Iraq. Problems are attributed to the age of the

weapons, as most of the SAWS are more than 10 years old and quite worn out.

A solution emerged in the form of FN Manufacturing's Mark 46 special-purpose weapon (SPW), a lightweight variation of the M249 SAW developed to meet a U.S. Special Operations requirement retaining the functionality and reliability of the standard model. Initially, the weapon was designed as the MK46 standard model, followed by the paratrooper variation with a shorter barrel and tubular

continued on page 54

Smoke drifts from the **M240** machine gun after it lays down a base of fire onto an enemy bunker and elements of the assault team use individual movement techniques (IMT) on the objective. The assistant gunner will change the heated barrel after several hundred rounds are fired to avoid damage to the barrel.

The Remington pump 870 shotgun helps Rangers of the 75th Ranger Regiment breach doorways and windows in an urban scenario. The custom sling is made out of 550-cord to the shooter's preferred length.

Weapons of the elite ranger unit are nothing ordinary these days. In light of the global war on terrorism, rapid fielding initiatives are implemented to bring the latest technology to these modern warriors.

Carl Gustav

The manufacturer of the Carl Gustav, Bofors, (Karlskoga, Sweden) is owned by United Defense Company based in Arlington, Virginia. Bofors dates back to the seventeenth century as an extensive producer of iron, more than any other plant in Sweden, and as manufacturer of cannons. The name Bofors is strongly associated with a 40mm antiaircraft gun based upon a Bofors design. The Allied Forces of World War II referred to this weapon as a Bofors gun and it became so widely known that any antiaircraft guns of the era were generally referred to as Bofors guns. The iron manufacturing company acquired its name from a small nearby creek in Sweden.

The Karl Gustaf Stads Gevarsfaktoriet (Carl Gustav's City Rifle Factory), a division of Bofors, made the light infantry rifle now referred to as a Swedish Mauser by North American gun collectors and enthusiasts. This factory continuously manufactured light infantry rifles from 1898 until 1925, and then intermittently produced them into the 1930s. In 1940, the rifle factory began development of recoilless weapons with reduced weight and recoil, and with high-velocity and small-caliber ammunition. Initially, the weapon appeared to be no more than a promising sniper rifle. Further experimentation increased the ammunition caliber to the already produced 20mm and 40mm. Influenced by antiarmor launchers such as the Bazooka and German-made World War II weaponry, the rifle gradually evolved into the 84mm Carl Gustav recoilless rifle that was initially introduced in 1946.

The M4A1 rifle with an M203 grenade launcher. The laser range/sight for the M203 is an add-on item. It makes the M4 top heavy and can get caught up in a Ranger's equipment when running or practicing individual movement techniques (IMTs).

The M4A1 rifle (top) with M203 grenade launcher, AN/PEQ-2 infrared pointer and illuminator, with the Aimpoint Comp-M sighting system is considerably heavier and more complex than the shotgun. The laser range finders help place deadly accurate fire onto a target. The Remington pump 870 shotgun with a snap link as a sling attaches to the shooter's assault vest and is used for breaching doors and windows.

A young Ranger peers down the sight of the Aimpoint Comp-M. This sight is not officially included in the special operations peculiar modification (SOPMOD) kit but is used throughout the regiment because of its close-quarter-combat red-dot sighting system that allows for the two-eyes-open method of sighting.

Room to room is the only way to clear a building or house in an urban environment with the threat of enemy combatants inside. After clearing several rooms, the fire team withdraws by teams. As one team moves back to the initial entrance point, the other team pulls security. This structure was specifically built for training purposes.

telescoped buttstock. The MK46 paratrooper model traded off some of the range and firepower for the desired compactness and maneuverability. The MK46 SPW variant was designed for the Rangers and special operations forces. It features an ergonomic non-folding plastic butt-stock, a barrel of intermediate length (between the standard and paratrooper models), and a Picatinny-type rail mount on the heat shield that accommodates a variety of mounted sights, scopes, laser designators, and flash-lights. It also has a forward pistol grip and a detachable bipod. To decrease its weight, the magazine-feed option of the standard and paratrooper models has been discarded. The MK46 is a gas-operated, air-cooled weapon equipped with disintegrating belts of standard NATO 5.56mm rounds. The belt can be fed from separate boxes or clip-on combat pouches of 100 rounds. The barrel detaches quickly and has a carrying handle to assist in replacing hot barrels.

With a retractable buttstock and an Aimpoint Comp-M sight, this MK48 gunner prepares for a mission to clear rooms on an objective. The Rangers' white light will be used because of the daylight pouring in through the objective's windows.

Claymore Mine
Weight: 1.58 kilograms
Length: 8 inches (216mm)
Width: 1.3 inches (35mm)
Height: 3 inches (83mm)

The MK48 is a big brother, or a scaled-up version of the 5.56mm MK46 light machine gun, an updated variant of the famous M249 SAW. Both the MK46 and the MK48 were developed for U.S. Special Forces, led by the U.S. Navy.

The M240G medium-class machine gun fires standard NATO 7.62mm ammunition and is used for support fire. The crew-served weapon has a removable barrel that can be changed easily to prevent overheating. The weapon has an integral folding bipod and can be mounted on a folding tripod for greater stability. When mounted, its maximum effective range is 1.8 kilometers. This machine gun has a cyclic rate of fire between 650 and 950 rounds per minute, depending on the regulator setting. Each ranger battalion was allotted 27 M240G machine guns to replace the older M60-series machine gun in the mid-1990s. The M60 7.62-mm machine gun had been the U.S. Army's general-purpose medium machine gun beginning in the late 1950s. Commonly referred to as the "hog" or "pig" by its operators, the M60 served as the primary machine gun for the

The new MK48 machine gun fires belt-fed A131 NATO 7.62mm rounds. The MK48 can also accommodate M80 4-ball M62 1-tracer links. The weapon is now in the 75th Ranger Regiment's inventory. This new lightweight weapon can move with the assault elements instead of remaining on the support. It gives ranger squads more firepower at the point of attack.

After a long night of movement and little sleep, Rangers engage targets from a standing position after kicking in a door and clearing the objective. The MK46 5.56mm machine gun has a forward vertical grip that attaches to the Picatinny rail interface system.

During a live-fire training exercise at Fort Campbell, Kentucky, a 1st Battalion Ranger dismounts from a ground mobility vehicle (GMV) and reacts to enemy contact. The Ranger is armed with a 7.62mm MK48 rifle complete with a Picatinny rail interface system. The Ranger is protected with Wiley X eye protection and a ballistic modular information communications helmet (MICH). He carries additional ammunition in his small assault pack and water in the CamelBak strapped to his back. SOCOM

Loading up for the mission and protected by the modular information communications helmet (MICH), Oakley eye protection, Nomax gloves, and knee pads, the Rangers are among the best-equipped soldiers in the world.

Rangers in the Vietnam War. In the mid-1970s, the 1st and 2nd Ranger Battalions mounted the M60 to a pintle on their jeeps, one on a center post pintle and occasionally one at a second location for use by the front passenger. The M60 continued service in the ranger regiment through 1993 with Task Force Ranger in Somalia. Like its descendants, the M60 fires standard NATO 7.62mm ammunition and is crewed by a two-man team, the shooter and the ammunition bearer. It has a removable barrel that can be changed to prevent overheating. The weapon has an integral folding bipod and can be mounted on a folding tripod.

The MK48 is a 7.62mm lightweight machine gun developed to meet the Rangers and special operations forces requirement for a lightweight and updated version

Below: Still called a SAW gunner, although the M249 SAW is no longer in use in the 75th Ranger Regiment, the MK46 has a plastic 200-round drum of 5.56mm ammunition just like the M249. The MK46 is usually mounted with a Trijicon advanced combat optical gun sight (ACOG) 4-power scope to engage targets at further distances than the Aimpoint Comp-M sight.

After sending a round down range at an enemy target, the 84mm Carl Gustav's gunner looks at the rest of the support element. The assistant gunner uses Steiner binoculars to assess the damage on the targets.

The commander of A Company, 3rd Battalion, briefs a squad before continuing on a live-fire lane exercise. Rangers carry all that they need on their assault vest, including the flex cuffs, an infrared (IR) chemical light for movement at night, and a CamelBak on-the-move hydration system. On the assault vest near the nape of the neck there is a reinforced loop with the soldier's name. This loop enables a fellow Ranger to grab a hold of his buddy in an emergency.

A Company Rangers from 1st Battalion react to enemy contact. This member of the weapons platoon has expended all the blank rounds in his 84mm Carl Gustav and must use his back-up weapon, the Colt M4. SOCOM

of the 7.62mm M240 machine gun that maintained the necessary firepower advantages and functionality of the previous model. Like the M240, the MK48's purpose in the ranger battalions is to provide sustained support fire for long-range-fire missions. The MK48's parts are compatible with the M240 and MK46 machine guns, and the MK48 boasts a Picatinny rail mounting system (one on the top of the receiver, four on the barrel) that accepts a variety of sights. The MK48 is fitted with open sights. Although only fielded since 2003, the MK48 has already proven its

Javelin

Manufacturer: Lockheed Martin Corporation
Range: 2,500 meters
Guidance: Passive target acquisition/fire control with integrated day/thermal sight
Magnification: 4x day; 4x or 9x thermal
Warhead: Tandem-shaped charge
Missile weight: 21.6 pounds (11.8 kilograms)
Command launch unit (CLU) weight: 14.1 pounds (6.4 kilograms)
Missile length: 42.6 inches (108.1 centimeters)
Launch tube length: 47.2 inches (119.8 centimeters)
Missile diameter: 5 inches (12.7 centimeters)
Launch tube diameter: 5.6 inches (14.2 centimeters)

During live-fire training, Rangers fire the 84mm Carl Gustav. The backblast creates a cloud of light. A two-man team operates this weapon system.

Rangers from the weapons platoon of A Company, 1st Battalion, are deployed to Fort Campbell, Kentucky, to participate in field training. The gunner prepares to fire the 84mm Carl Gustav weapon from the shoulder as the assistant gunner (right) loads the weapon. The assistant gunner stands clear of the weapon's backblast, and both Rangers wear hearing protection. Gillian M. Albro, USASOC PAO

The 84mm Carl Gustav, or ranger antitank weapon system (RAWS), can fire high explosive (HE), high explosive antitank (HEAT) with illumination, and smoke rounds. A flechétte round is also manufactured but sees little use in the ranger regiment.

reliability compared to the M60 machine gun. Initially built for the SEALs, the MK48 is used in conjunction with the medium, mounted M240 machine gun. Rangers increase their firepower during a mission by maintaining M240s on the ranger ground mobility vehicles and carrying the 7.62mm Mark 48 when they dismount.

The MK48 is a gas-operated, air-cooled, belt-fed machine gun that uses standard disintegrating 7.62mm belts. It is fitted with an under-barrel gas system and a rotating bolt locking system. Its special operations forces features are very similar to the smaller MK46 SPW: ammunition can be fed from separate boxes or clip-on combat pouches of 100 rounds, the barrel detaches quickly and has a carrying handle to assist with replacement of hot barrels. The solid, non-folding plastic buttstock is ergonomically designed. The MK48 has a folding integral bipod and a carrying sling.

ANTITANK WEAPON SYSTEMS

Ranger units have a limited antiarmor capability. The 84mm Carl Gustav, also referred to as the ranger antitank weapon system (RAWS), is unique to the ranger battalions and is gaining widespread use in light infantry units

Tired, wet, and hungry members of the 3rd Ranger Battalion prepare by training under harsh conditions. Intense training prepares them physically, emotionally, and mentally for the harrowing deployments to the Middle East. The men have been training for two days straight with little-to-no sleep and two meals ready-to-eat (MRE) a day.

internationally. The Carl Gustav is becoming a favorite with SEAL units as well. This crew-served versatile weapon can fire high explosive (HE) and high explosive antitank (HEAT) rounds, illumination rounds, and smoke rounds. The weapon's effective range varies between 200 and 1,300 meters depending upon its type of ammunition. The weapon is currently used to combat concrete bunkers, heavy armor, armored personnel carriers, and aircraft.

The Carl Gustav weighs in at 25 pounds and is 42 inches long. Two Rangers, the gunner and the loader, are needed to operate the Carl Gustav. The gunner ports, aims, and fires the weapon. The second man reloads, provides covering fire if necessary, and transports spare rounds. The 84mm Carl Gustav can be fired from the shoulder, while standing, while kneeling, or from a prone position with an M2 tripod. The ammunition is encased in an expendable, single-piece, fiberglass-wrapped tube. Ammunition resembles fin-stabilized rocket-type cartridges.

The key to the RAWS' versatility is a new generation of highly effective ammunition. The HEAT 751 round has the combined effect of an explosively formed penetrator and a hollow charge. It strikes and penetrates explosive reactive armor (ERA) tiles without initiating them, and its main charge blasts through the armored protection leaving massive internal damage. It penetrates armor up to 500 millimeters thick. The HEAT 551 round knocks out approximately 90 percent of all armored vehicles at ranges of up to 700 meters. It is highly effective against other hard targets, such as concrete bunkers, landing craft, and aircraft. It has an armored penetration of 400 millimeters. The HE 441B round can be set to an impact detonation or an air burst detonation. This high-explosive round combats troops in the open or behind cover and engages soft-skinned vehicles and similar targets. It has a maximum range of 1,100 meters. The HEDP 502 round is a dual- or combined-purpose HE and HEAT round optimized for combat in urban areas. It is effective against light armored vehicles, concrete and brick walls, field fortifications, and ground forces. The Illuminating 545 round rapidly illuminates target areas and helps ground forces complete their mission. It has a maximum range of 2,100

A Ranger trains on an MK19 grenade launcher while deployed in support of Operation Enduring Freedom (OEF) in Afghanistan. Prior to a mission, Rangers test fire their weapons within a secured area. SOCOM

The Javelin is so technologically advanced that it can trace a target with its sighting system, displace and move to another position, or bring the weapon back up to the fire position, and the round will still trace the initial target and engage it. The Javelin is a fire-and-forget weapon, but the sighting system is not. Quite costly, the sighting is ironically transported in a canvas aviator's kit bag at times.

meters. The Smoke 469B round develops a smoke screen instantaneously upon impact. For target practice, the 84mm TP 552 round is ballistically matched to the 84mm HEAT 551 round but carries an inert warhead.

The special operations command continually seeks to improve its soldier-carried demolition weapons to include a multi-target warhead that can take out light armor, a bunker, or a triple brick wall (the equivalent of 12 inches of

Mounted on a desert mobility vehicle, this MK19 grenade launcher is fitted with an AN/PEQ-2 illuminator and laser pointer for accurate target engagement.

concrete). More specifically, United States forces need a weapon or ammunition that will engage specific and deeply imbedded tunnel targets with a maximum elimination of personnel and equipment to be used in the tunnels and caves of Afghanistan. Already in the United States forces' arsenal, a thermo-baric variant of the Hellfire missile has destroyed bunkers and buildings during the conflict in Iraq. Translating this weaponry concept to a portable shoulder-fired weapon that is based on a new class of solid fuel-air explosive thermo-barics gives the Rangers the advantage against al Qaeda and Taliban forces in Afghanistan's mountain ranges. This warhead is filled with an advanced thermo-baric explosive that, when detonated, generates high sustained-blast pressures in confined spaces. The Carl Gustav with thermo-baric munitions provides the necessary firepower to the ranger battalions in Afghanistan and the Tora Bora caves.

The Javelin and Stinger are also shoulder-fired portable guided-missile weapons designed to engage tracked, wheeled, or amphibious vehicles. They are also effective against low-altitude jets, fixed-wing aircraft, helicopters, unmanned aerial vehicles, and cruise missiles. Each system is designed as a fire-and-forget weapon, which aids in keeping the Rangers' load light. After the missile is expended, the empty weapon system is discarded.

The Stinger missile system provides the Rangers with force protection mostly against airborne targets such as fixed-wing aircraft, helicopters, unmanned aerial vehicles, and cruise missiles. The system employs a passive infrared seeker and proportional navigation system. It is designed for continued and future uses with an all-aspect engagement capability and with identification-friend-or-foe (IFF) for improved range and maneuverability. The Stinger launches from a number of platforms like the ranger special operations vehicle (RSOV) or desert patrol vehicle (DPV). The missile, packaged within its disposable launch tube, is delivered as a certified round, requiring no field testing or direct-support maintenance. A separable, reusable grip stock is attached to the round prior to using the weapon.

The Javelin is a portable antitank weapon that can also engage covered targets, bunkers, buildings, and stationary or slow-moving helicopters. A full system weighs 49.5 pounds, and its missiles have a range of 2,500 meters. The system is deployed and ready to fire in less than 30 seconds, and the reload time is less than 20 seconds. Reloading requires the Ranger to attach the loaded pre-assembled launch tube to the command launch unit. The launch tube assembly is discarded after firing the missile. The missile is equipped with an imaging infrared (IR) seeker. The IR image allows the Ranger to identify enemy armor targets. Javelin gunners must identify battlefield

The MK19 fires a 40mm grenade that delivers significant damage to its target. Rangers demonstrate proficiency on all weapon systems available to the men of the ranger regiment. This promotes teamwork and interdependability among the soldiers.

The Javelin is an essential and significant weapon system for the Rangers. It comes in two parts, the warhead and the optics. It is a one-time-fire weapon, but the sight/optics can be recovered and used again.

combatants and distinguish friend from foe at night based on the images seen in the night-vision equipment.

All of the Javelin gunner controls for the missile system are on the command launch unit (CLU). The CLU, powered by a disposable battery, provides the capability for battle-field surveillance, target acquisition, missile launch, and damage assessment.

The Javelin missile system features "lock on before launch" and automatic self-guidance. The Ranger engages the target using the sight on the CLU and then locks onto the target with the automatic target tracker in the missile. When the system is locked on, the missile is ready to fire, and the Ranger does not carry out post-launch tracking or missile guidance. Unlike conventional wire-guided, fiber-optic-cable-guided, or laser-beam-riding missiles, the Javelin is autonomously guided to the target after launch, leaving the Ranger gunner free to take

cover, avoid counter fire, reposition, reload immediately, or continue his mission. The Javelin's soft-launch design feature allows employment from within buildings and enclosed fighting positions. The soft-launch option limits the gunner's exposure to the enemy.

The weapon has two attack modes: direct or top attack. The gunner selects direct-attack mode to engage covered targets, bunkers, buildings, and helicopters. The missile is launched at an 18-degree elevation angle to reach a peak altitude of 50 meters in direct-fire mode. The top-attack mode is selected against tanks, in which case the Javelin climbs above and strikes down on top of the target to penetrate the roof of the tank, the area with the least amount of armored protection. The missile is launched at an 18-degree elevation angle to reach a peak altitude of 150 meters in top-attack mode. The Javelin boasts significant reliability and a 94-percent probability of engagement on the first firing.

Rangers also employ the light antitank weapon (LAW) from the M72-series weaponry and the AT4; both are lightweight, shoulder-fired antiarmor weapons. The LAW, initially developed in the 1960s by Talley Industries under license in Norway, is a self-contained antitank weapon consisting of a 66mm rocket packed in a launcher. It is issued with a round of ammunition. The launcher, which consists of one tube inside the other, serves as a water-tight packing container for the rocket and houses a percussion-type firing mechanism that activates the

A Ranger can take out anything with the Javelin. No countermeasures, antimissile weapons, or reactive armor have been developed to combat the power and advanced technology of this weapon. The warhead seeks and sends target information to its sensor, which finds the weakest point to engage on the target.

rocket. The LAW may be fired from either shoulder and requires minimal operator knowledge and operator maintenance. The launcher must be extended prior to firing. Weighing in at approximately 5 pounds, a single soldier can port and operate this lethal weapon.

The special operations command is hastening to add close-quarters capability to the M72 LAW for the U.S. Army Rangers and the 160th Special Operations Aviation Regiment (Airborne). The LAW close support (LAW-CS) is a recoilless, shoulder-fired antiarmor and breaching weapon designed to operate in urban areas without harming the operator. The LAW-CS is meant to correct the problems of the current LAW and its recurring safety problems during close-support use.

The M136 AT4 is a recoilless rifle used primarily by the ranger battalion and other infantry forces for engagement of light armored tanks. The AT4's round of ammunition is self-contained in a disposable, one-piece, fiberglass-wrapped launch tube. The free-flight, fin-stabilized, rocket-type cartridge is an 84mm high explosive antiarmor explosive capable of penetrating 14 inches (35.6 centimeters) of armor. The portable system weighs 15 pounds and can be utilized effectively with minimal training. Unlike the M72-series LAW, the AT4 launcher does not need to be extended prior to firing. The M136 AT4 fires from the right shoulder only. Like the LAW, the AT4 launcher is watertight for easy transportation and storage.

The MK19 grenade machine gun can fire a variety of 40mm grenades at over 350 grenades per minute with a maximum range of over 2,200 meters. The MK19 fires six types of cartridges: M430I/M430A1 high explosive dual-purpose (HEDP) grenades, M383 high explosive grenades, M385I/M918 training practice, and M922/M922A1 dummy rounds. The M430 HEDP 40mm grenade can pierce armor up to 2 inches thick and produce fragments to kill personnel within 5 meters of the point of impact and wound personnel within 15 meters of the point of impact. The grenade launcher, with its cradle and tripod, weighs about 137 pounds and is usually found mounted to desert- or ground-mobility vehicles. It is transportable over short distances with limited amounts of ammunition. The MK19 40mm Mod 3 machine gun is an air-cooled, disintegrating metallic-link-belt-fed, blowback-operated, fully automatic weapon. Each ranger battalion is allotted 12 of these grenade launchers. Initially developed by the U.S. Navy in the early 1960s, modifications to the MK19 have improved its performance and have allowed Rangers and other special forces units in the army to deploy the MK19 in the harshest environments encountered in their operations worldwide.

The 60mm M224 lightweight company mortar system provides the ranger company commander with indirect fire support for an entire company element. With its maximum effective range of approximately 3,500 meters (just over 2 miles), the M224 engages targets at the outer limits of the

MK19 Mod 3 40mm Grenade Machine Gun

Primary function: Mounted antiarmor weapon
Manufacturer: Saco Defense Industries
Length: 43.1 inches (109.47 centimeters)
Total weight: 137.5 pounds (62.43 kilograms)
Gun weight: 72.5 pounds (32.92 kilograms)
Cradle (MK64 Mod 5) weight: 21.0 pounds (9.53 kilograms)
Tripod weight: 44.0 pounds (19.98 kilograms)
Muzzle velocity: 790 feet (240.69 meters) per second
Bore diameter: 40mm
Maximum range: 2,200 meters
Maximum effective range: 1,600 meters
Cyclic rate of fire: 325 to 375 rounds per min.
Rapid rate of fire: 60 rounds per minute
Sustained rate of fire: 40 rounds per minute

a base plate with elevating mechanisms that enable the M224 to attack at a high angle of fire. It can be fired while mounted on the base plate or from the hand-held position. The M224 features a spring shock absorber to absorb the recoil. The M64A1 sight is self-illuminating for night operations. The M64 sight unit attaches to the bipod mount via a standard dovetail. An additional short-range sight attaches to the base of the cannon tube to fire the mortar on the move and during assaults.

Tactical ammunition options for the M224 include: high explosive/multi-option fuse, high explosive/point-detonating fuse, white phosphorous/smoke, and illumination. The M720 and M888 high-explosive cartridges designed for the 60mm M224 mortar system are employed against personnel, bunkers, and light material targets. The high-fragmentation steel projectile is loaded with composition B explosive. The M720 and M888 high explosives are identical with the exception of the fuse. The M720 is equipped with a multi-option fuse that can be set to function in proximity, near surface burst, impact, or delay mode. The M888 is equipped with a point-detonating fuse that functions in the impact mode only.

The M224 60mm mortar is the smallest and lightest of the Rangers' mortar tubes.

company zone of influence. Relatively small at 46 1/2 pounds and 40 inches in length, the M224 is well suited for light infantry and special operations forces like the Rangers. The four 60mm mortars in each battalion are crew-served weapons. Typically, three Rangers implement the mortar system.

The M224 60mm mortar replaced the older World War II–era 60mm mortars. These dated weapons possessed 2,200 yards of effective range. The M224 was designed to fire all types of ammunition, but of primary importance, its rounds have a longer range.

Ammunition is typically dropped, base end first, into a smooth cannon muzzle. A firing pin at the bottom of the gun tube initiates the primer, which then ignites the propellant. The expanding gas from the burning propellant initiates the round. It can be trigger fired by a manual spring-loaded firing system. This mortar system boasts a maximum rate of fire of 30 rounds per minute and a sustained rate of fire of 20 rounds per minute. The mount consists of a bipod and

M249 Squad Automatic Weapons System (SAWS)

Primary function: Hand-held combat machine gun

Manufacturer: Fabrique Nationale (FN Herstal) Manufacturing, Inc.

Length: 40.87 inches (103.81 centimeters)

Weight with bipod and tools: 15.16 pounds (6.88 kilograms)

Weight with 200-round box magazine: 6.92 pounds (3.14 kilograms)

Weight with 30-round magazine: 1.07 pounds (0.49 kilograms)

Bore diameter: 5.56mm (0.233 inches)

Maximum effective range: 3,281 feet (1,000 meters) for an area target

Maximum range: 2.23 miles (3.6 kilometers)

Cyclic rates of fire: 725 rounds per minute

Sustained rates of fire: 85 rounds per minute

The **M224 60mm mortar** is the ranger regiment's most commonly used mortar. It can provide devastating damage to bunkers, vehicles, and outposts.

MK46 SPW	MK48 SPW
Caliber:	
5.56x45mm NATO	7.62x51mm NATO
Weight empty:	
12.6 pounds	18.64 pounds
Length overall:	
35.75 inches	39.75 inches
Barrel length:	
16 inches	19.75 inches
Feeding:	
Belt only	Belt only
Cyclic rate of fire:	
750 rounds per minute	710 rounds per minute
Range:	
3,600 meters (maximum)	800 (maximum)

Lasting Tradition of Firearms

Fabrique Nationale d'Armes de Guerre was established in 1889 to manufacture 150,000 Mauser rifles ordered by the Belgian government. Serving the military's needs has been the foundation for the company. In 1898, Fabrique Nationale d'Armes de Guerre (later referred to as FN Herstal) entered into a long-lasting relationship with John Moses Browning, a leader of innovative firearms design. Together, FN and Mr. Browning produced several of the most prestigious weapons in the world, including the 9mm Hi-Power Pistol and Browning machine guns. FN Herstal's headquarters are located in the city of Herstal, Belgium, in the heart of Europe. Facilities in Europe and the United States are equipped with state-of-the-art machinery, prestigious firearms designers, and professionally trained technicians.

The **120mm** is the largest of the three mortar systems employed by the ranger regiment. With rounds large enough to take out a city block, it packs indirect fire into a semi-portable system.

Browning M2 .50-caliber Machine Gun

Primary function: Automatic weapon, suppressive fire for offensive and defensive purposes
Manufacturer: Ramo Defence in United States, FN Herstal Manufacturing, Inc. in Belgium
Length: 61.42 inches (156 centimeters)
Gun weight: 84 pounds (38 kilograms)
Lightweight version: 60 pounds (27 kilograms)
M3 tripod (complete) weight: 44 pounds (19.98 kilograms)
Total weight: 128 pounds (58 kilograms)
Bore diameter: 0.50 inches (12.7x99mm)
Maximum effective range: 2,000 meters with tripod mount
Maximum range: 4.22 miles (6.8 kilometers)
Maximum effective range: 1,830 meters
Cyclic rate of fire: 550 rounds per minute

The M2 machine gun on the M3 tripod provides a stable firing platform that, combined with the slow rate of fire and the traversing and elevating mechanism, provides ground soldiers with another offensive possibility. During the Vietnam War, the M2 was used as a sniper weapon at fixed installations such as firebases. Snipers pre-fired the weapon at identifiable targets and worked the data into range cards, ensuring increased first-round accuracy. This practice was used to a very limited extent.

The Rangers simply call it a slap round—the M903 .50-caliber saboted light armor penetrator (SLAP) ammunition was developed by the U.S. Marine Corps during the 1980s and approved for service use in 1990 during Operation Desert Storm. With a firing velocity of 3,985 feet per second and a maximum effective range of 1,500 meters, this round maximizes the Browning M2 .50-caliber machine gun's effectiveness in engagement and defeat of light armored targets. The SLAP round has demonstrated increased armor penetration over other ammunition options in the field. This is how it works: The round is a reduced-caliber heavy metal (like tungsten) penetrator of 0.30 inches diameter. It is wrapped in a smooth plastic or nylon-like sabot (shoe) now totaling 0.50 inches diameter. The slick sides of the sabot offer very little resistance in the machine gun's barrel. Also, the mass of the SLAP round is much lighter than the normal 0.50-caliber round, thus increasing the SLAP round's velocity and flat trajectory. The combination of velocity and flat trajectory increases the hit probability. The SLAP ammunition is completely interoperable with unmodified M2 machine guns with Stellite liner.

The word *sabot*, derived from the French and probably of Turkish or Arabic origin, refers to a wooden shoe worn in some European countries, especially in rural areas and by working people. French workers used to show their protest against employers with knocking and walking noisily in their sabots. It is said that sometimes sabots were thrown into factory machinery in riotous acts to damage it. While *sabot* can mean a wooden shoe, it can also mean a metal shoe or clamp for holding a piece of metal in place. Striking French railway workers would cut the metal shoe or *sabot* that held railroad tracks in place. This practice points to the origin of *sabotage*.

The U.S. Army Research, Development, and Engineering Center at Picatinny Arsenal has developed and recently fielded the first XM32 lightweight hand-held mortar ballistic computers (LHMBCs), essentially rugged personal computers. The Stryker brigade combat teams (SBCT) in Iraq had an urgent need for such computers, and funding profiles expect the fielding of 30 LHMBC systems to the 75th Ranger Regiment in the spring of 2005.

The XM32 is a ballistic calculator that automates a number of different procedures, such as determining ammunition requirements for a given target and calculating firing orders for large target areas in terms of traverse.

According to David Super, the deputy product manager for mortar systems at Picatinny Arsenal, the new XM32 mortar ballistic computer weighs less than 2 pounds and swiftly calculates the ballistic solution for mortar systems, including the 60mm, 81mm, and 120mm mortar weapons and their complete inventory of ammunition.

David Super explains that the current hand-held mortar ballistic computer is the 8-pound M23, which was built in the 1970s and is equivalent to the outdated Commodore 64 computers. At this time, the M23 is obsolete, cannot be repaired, and cannot be expanded to accommodate new ammunition options.

The newly fielded XM32 supports all current fielded mortar ammunition and features expanded software to allow for the incorporation of any future mortar rounds. It provides Rangers with a more accurate solution, based on a ballistic algorithm that accounts for wind speed, wind temperature, and propellant temperature. Since the current M23 software does not account for all of today's ammunition options, Rangers must manually calculate with triangulation methods, which consumes more time. With the XM32, Rangers can be more responsive, timely, and accurate.

This cleverly improvised field-expedient breaching device is made by taking a fence post or a 1x2-inch board and securing C4 explosives to it with 100-mile-per-hour tape. The Ranger slides it into, or places it on top of, a wire obstacle. The fuse is pulled, and it will detonate within the time it takes the fuse to reach the explosives.

The M722 smoke cartridge is designed as a spotting/marking round. The steel projectile is loaded with bulk white phosphorus. The smoke cartridge is equipped with a point-detonating fuse that functions in the impact mode. When the fuse is triggered, a burst ruptures the projectile and disperses the white phosphorus smoke.

The illumination round enhances night-vision capabilities for soldiers by illuminating target areas to facilitate adjustment of fire. The projectile is loaded with candle and parachute assemblies. When the fuse functions, it initiates the two assemblies and, as the parachute deploys, the candle burns, providing the required illumination over the target area. The M721 and M767 illumination rounds are identical with the exception of the candle composition. The M721 contains a standard illuminant mix that provides approximately 300,000 candlepower of light. The newer M767 contains an infrared illuminant mix that provides approximately 75 watts of infrared light with less than 350 candlepower of visible light. The M767 was designed for use with night-vision devices. The M767 illumination rounds provide infrared illumination to the full range of the M720 HE cartridge, up to 2 miles. The illumination rounds are equipped with a mechanical time fuse, which initiates the fuse at a user-specified time after the launch. These rounds burst at 425 meters and burn for 55 seconds.

The M766 short-range practice cartridge is designed for realistic and cost-effective training with the M224 60mm mortar system. The M766 is similar to the 60mm high-explosive cartridge in exterior configuration and operation. The cartridge has a maximum range of 538 meters and provides a flash, bang, and smoke upon impact. With the use of a refurbishment kit, the M766 practice cartridge can be re-fired between 10 and 24 times.

Ranger battalions also use the M29A1 and M259 versions of the 81mm mortar, a crew-served, indirect-fire weapon that offers a maximum effective range of 5,700 meters. The 81mm mortar weighs just less than 90 pounds. The M120 and M121 are heavy mortars with a 120mm round that provides a high angle of fire to support ground troops. Weighing in at nearly 320 pounds, it is transported by a vehicle specifically rigged for the heavy mortar.

OTHER EXPLOSIVE OPTIONS

The army's special operations forces have performed demolition operations dating back before World War II using bulk explosives and non-standard, improvised methods. Soldiers have used found materials such as scrap wood, glass champagne bottle bottoms, and steel plates, molding the explosive to the items in an attempt to increase the efficiency of the charges for specialized missions.

Stinger Missile

Primary function: To provide close-in, surface-to-air weapons for defense
Primer manufacturer: Hughes Missile System Company
Missile manufacturer: General Dynamics/Raytheon Corporation
Propulsion: Dual-thrust solid-fuel rocket motor
Length: 5 feet (1.5 meters)
Width: 5.5 inches (13.96 centimeters)
Unarmed weight: 12.5 pounds (5.68 kilograms)
Fully armed weight: 34.5 pounds (15.66 kilograms)
Range: 1 to 8 kilometers
Rate of fire: 1 missile every 3 to 7 seconds
Crew: 2

Since the advent of munitions incorporating explosively formed penetrators (EFP) as warheads, the special operations forces have learned to build demolition charges using this technology. In addition to fabricating the charges, soldiers must improvise methods to attach the charges to a wide variety of targets, often for extended periods of time, in virtually all environmental conditions. The attachment methods require the soldier's direct presence at the target, which could be a bridge's support columns, an electrical power substation, etc. Many of these missions do not permit a safe standoff distance from the target during placement of the demolition charges. This exposes the soldiers to detection and eradication by the enemy forces.

The M303 special operations forces demolition kit (SOFDK) is a collection of inert metal parts, plastic parts, and commercially available items that give the Rangers a wide selection of warheads and attachment devices they can tailor to defeat a specific mission target. The various warheads include three sizes of conical-shaped charges, four sizes of linear-shaped charges, and two sizes of lightweight explosively formed penetrators (EFP).

Claymore mines and bangalore torpedoes are explosives that have remained relatively constant in their design for decades. The claymore mine is favored by special operations units. Developed after the Korean War, the M18A1 claymore is nothing more than a small charge of C4 explosive packed behind 700 steel balls. When the C4 is ignited, the balls are shot out in a forward 60-degree pattern. Its effective range is 50 meters. In the presence of jungle, trees, buildings, or other obstacles, the radius of impact will vary.

A soldier can either place the claymore against a solid object or stand it up on its four legs that allow it to anchor into the ground. One hundred feet of cable connects the mine to an M57 triggering device, better known as the hell box. After placing the charge, the soldier retreats from the mine's location and the cable is strung back to the defensive position. In many cases, Vietnam War–era soldiers positioned two claymores side by side to create an increased spray of shrapnel. The claymore is moderately waterproof. Remarkably, it can function under water for at least two hours.

The M1A1 bangalore torpedo is an antipersonnel mine-clearing charge that dates back to the 1940s and World War II. The bangalore is effective in clearing minefields and breaching barbed-wired areas, but is less effective in cutting today's high-tensile-strength barbed-wired obstacles. Each bangalore section weighs 13 pounds,

Tossing grenades into a 15-meter circle from 50 feet away is the standard necessary to get a "go" during expert infantryman's badge (EIB) testing. The grenade has a kill radius of 5 meters.

including 9 pounds of explosives. The bangalore kit consists of ten 5-foot sections, and is awkward and heavy for light infantry Rangers to transport. To utilize this explosive, the sections are connected and pushed through the minefield before detonating. An electric or non-electric blasting cap initiates detonation.

Although bangalore torpedoes are available in a kit, Rangers may improvise with a more homemade arrangement. Sections of fencing or wooden planks found in the field are often packed with C4, wrapped with 100-mile-per-hour tape or secured with flex cuffs, and detonated with a blasting cap. Such an explosive can clear a lane 1 meter in width, allowing Rangers to breach a barbed-wire obstacle, for example.

Selectable lightweight attack munition (SLAM) is antimaterial and antivehicular munition that is light, compact, and effective. For the ranger battalion, it replaces the M15, M19, and M21 antitank mines. SLAM is designed to destroy enemy vehicles such as parked aircraft and hard- and soft-armored vehicles, ammunition and petroleum sites, storage facilities, and other targets, all while avoiding direct contact with the enemy. It is used to support hit-and-run, ambush, and urban warfare missions. The SLAM has four possible methods of detonation: mine function, trip wire, command or operator detonation, and time delay with an integral timer. This munition is easily portable in quantity, weighing in at only 2.2 pounds each.

Support from the Air

Austrian philosopher Christian von Ehrenfels published a paper in 1890 titled "On Gestalt Qualities," in which he determined that a melody is still recognizable when played in different keys, even though none of the notes are the same. Ehrenfels continued to argue that if a melody and the notes that comprise it are so independent, then a whole is not simply the sum of its parts, but a synergistic "whole effect," or gestalt.

On many occasions and for various reasons, officials separate the United States Army special operations forces units to analyze their successes and lessons learned on the battlefield. However, when deployed to the battlefront, the individual special operations forces elements seamlessly blend an interlocking weave with one another and other support systems, creating a dynamic interrelationship, a continuous melody, a gestalt. The elements of the 75th Ranger Regiment display their individuality and uniqueness in skill but cannot fully succeed without their counterparts in arms. Together, they fight the fight, thus creating a unified effect and an

Left: After conducting a raid on an enemy position, the assault elements are extracted by Black Hawks at a pickup zone and flown to the assembly area in a friendly/secure area. The support elements are the last to withdraw from the area. This Black Hawk has an in-flight refueling probe for lengthy missions.

The MH-60L Black Hawk direct-action penetrator (DAP) helicopter has several weapons configurations. Here it sports an M230 30mm chain gun capable of firing 625 rounds per minute. It has an effective range of 4,000 meters and fires high explosive dual-purpose (HEDP) munitions.

entity of insurmountable strength. The whole is far greater than the sum of its parts.

The 75th Ranger Regiment displays expansive battle-field diversity, conducting airborne and air assaults in harrowing mountain infiltrations, complex urban raids, and rescue operations. Assisting the Rangers in their mission is an extensive array of technologically advanced support elements, equipment, and training resources. No other asset is quite as instrumental in this task as the 160th Special Operations Aviation Regiment (Airborne), also known as 160th SOAR(A) or Task Force 160. Without Task Force 160, Rangers would not have the means to infiltrate enemy lines, receive quick fire support, or be rescued. Many of the successes enjoyed by the 75th Ranger Regiment throughout their history and during the present global war on terrorism are directly linked to the consistent relationship it has with Task Force 160.

After the United States' failed attempt to rescue hostages in Iran in April, 1980, the army began evaluating and developing the training resources to establish a special operations aviation unit that was prepared to

Black Hawk

UH-60A
UH-60L

Mass gross weight:
20,250 pounds
22,000 pounds, 23,500 (external cargo)

Cruise speed:
139 knots
150 knots

Endurance:
2.3 hours
2.1 hours

Max range:
320 nautical miles
306 nautical miles

External load:
8,000 pounds
9,000 pounds

Internal load:
2,640 pounds (or 11 combat-equipped troops)

Crew:
Four (two pilots; two crew chiefs)

Armament:
Two 7.62mm machine guns

Aviation Regiment (Airborne). The regiment is assigned to the United States Special Operations Command. This unit of specially trained army aviators receives its orders from the joint chiefs of staff, making them the Pentagon's elite asset. The unit's focus on nighttime operations resulted in their nickname, night stalkers.

Task Force 160 has responded to the increased demand for elite, highly trained special operations aviation assets and has earned a solid reputation in the special operations community as the unit that is always at the right place, at the right time, and with the right assets. The motto of the 160th SOAR(A) is simply, "night stalkers don't quit." Consistent with their special operations counterparts, Task Force 160 pushes forward to continue with a mission despite bad weather, equipment failure, or heavy enemy resistance.

The AH-6 and MH-6 Little Birds, MH-60 Black Hawks, and MH-47 Chinooks of the 160th SOAR(A) insert, extract, and support special operations forces behind enemy lines or within hostile areas. If a situation dictates insertion and extraction of troops by force, Task Force 160 will employ accurate helicopter attack capabilities and precise helicopter lifts. They put troops in or take them out of harm's way within 30 seconds of the scheduled time. Army Rangers and U.S. Navy SEAL teams are the primary recipients of their specialized aviation tactics and techniques, reliable air support, security, and resources.

Headquartered at Fort Campbell, Kentucky, the 160th SOAR(A)'s 1st and 2nd Battalions and Special Operations Aviation Training Company are stationed at Fort Campbell; the 3rd Battalion is located at Hunter Army Airfield near Savannah, Georgia. The 160th SOAR(A) also activated a separate detachment and incorporated one National Guard battalion. The organizational structure allows the 160th SOAR(A) Regiment to quickly tailor its assets to meet mission requirements of special operations forces. The 160th SOAR(A) keeps its aircraft ready to deploy with a four-hour notice.

All night stalkers are volunteers. The 160th SOAR(A) seeks the best-qualified aviators and support soldiers available in today's United States Army. Once assigned to the regiment, incoming officers and enlisted soldiers go through basic mission qualification. The officer qualification course lasts 14 weeks, while the enlisted qualification course is three weeks long. Two other aviator qualification levels exist: fully mission qualified and flight lead. Special operations aviation pilots and soldiers develop a train-as-you're-going-to-fight mentality. The men of the 160th fully understand that they will participate in combat missions.

The basic mission-qualified aviator can copilot on operational missions and continues training in one of the operational battalions. Pilots spend one to one-and-a-half

respond in a future crisis. The decision was made to form a standing army special operations aviation task force. Volunteers were selected from attachments of the 101st Aviation Battalion, 158th Aviation Battalion, 229th Aviation Battalion, and the 159th Aviation Battalion to form Task Force 158. These aviators engaged in intense night-flying training and developed the tactics, techniques, and procedures for aviation in the special operations mission. Task Force 158 evolved into Task Force 160, which was later designated as the official unit of the 160th Aviation Battalion in October, 1981. This unit gradually developed into the 160th Special Operations Aviation Group (Airborne) and later, in May, 1990, the 160th Special Operations

The Black Hawk helicopter is armed with a variety of weapon systems to provide close air support to ground troops. This minigun can deliver thousands of rounds per minute to enemy targets below. Black Hawk pilots are accustomed to flying aircraft in dangerous and hostile situations.

The first special operations Black Hawk was the MH-60A, an upgraded and modified UH-60. In the late 1980s, a newer version, called the MH-60L, was introduced. The MH-60L was partially through its final evaluation phase when Iraq invaded Kuwait. The upgrade process was accelerated and several of the L models served in Desert Storm along with the older MH-60A models. The MH-60L was to be the low end of the series and the then-unproduced MH-60K direct-action penetrator (DAP) version would become the pride of the Black Hawk family. The MH-60K DAP was the first to be designed from its inception specifically for special operations aviation missions. It was designed with input from pilots of the 160th Special Operations Aviation Regiment (Airborne).

Nicknamed "night stalkers" as a result of their uncanny ability to strike undetected during darkness, it is not unusual for Task Force 160 pilots to log more flight hours wearing night-vision goggles than during daylight hours. "There is nothing like the feeling you get when sitting on the skids of a Little Bird," one Ranger explains. "That eerie combination of mysterious darkness all around you and calmness with the whirl of the bird's rotors . . . the rushing wind rings in your ears . . . and just knowing we are flying up there, but not a soul knows it, hears us, or sees the Little Bird coming—it is quite a remarkable feeling."

A fast-rope insertion/extraction system (FRIES) is mounted on either side of the Black Hawk's body and each can support 1,500 pounds. In a matter of a few minutes, a ranger patrol can exit the aircraft, land on the ground, and move out to the objective.

The Boeing-made MH-47D Chinook helicopter transports troops, artillery, supplies, and equipment to the battlefield. Other roles include medical evacuation, aircraft recovery, parachute drop, search and rescue, disaster relief, firefighting, and heavy construction. One hundred sixty-three MH-47Ds took part in Operations Desert Shield and Desert Storm. Over 1,000 Chinooks are operational worldwide, with more than 480 MH-47 Chinooks in the United States Army and National Guard.

more years training and building experience in a 160th SOAR(A) battalion before becoming fully mission qualified to command an aircraft on an operational mission. Flight lead status is granted to only the most experienced aviators. This qualification follows after another three to four years of training and experience. Commissioned officers can be flight lead qualified, but more often, it is the warrant officers who take the pilot's seat of lead aircraft.

The 160th SOAR(A) battalions are organized to address the operational needs of the special operations unit they support, according to the expected theater of operations, type of mission, and level of conflict. To address their needs, state-of-the-art equipment is a critical requirement. The 160th SOAR(A) possesses a variety of capable aircraft, including MH-60 Black Hawk medium utility helicopters, MH–47 Chinook heavy helicopters, and A/MH-6 Little Bird light special operations helicopters. Each aircraft has a specific mission and purpose for the 75th Ranger Regiment.

LITTLE BIRDS

The AH-6 and MH-6 Little Bird helicopters are direct descendents of the OH-6A Cayuse light observation helicopters used during the Vietnam War. The AH-6 is an attack version used in close aerial support for ground

Rangers conduct final crew briefing with pilots of an MH-53 helicopter prior to a mission in support of Operation Enduring Freedom (OEF) in the mountains of eastern Afghanistan. In the rugged environment of Afghanistan, brown-outs were experienced by helicopter pilots landing. The pilots called it "rotor borealis," the lightshow put on by sand friction against the rotor blades. SOCOM

Chinook

Maximum gross weight:
50,000 pounds

Empty weight:
23,401 pounds

Max speed:
170 knots / 184 miles per hour

Normal cruise speed:
130 knots / 137 miles per hour

Rate of climb:
1,522 feet per minute

Rotor system:
Three manual-folding blades per hub (two hubs); 225 revolutions per minute; 60-foot rotor span

Troop capacity:
36 (33 troops plus three crew members)

Litter capacity:
24

Sling-load capacity:
26,000-pound center hook; 17,000-pound forward/aft hook; 25,000-pound tandem

Minimum crew:
Three (pilot, copilot, and flight engineer)

Rangers quickly move out to an MH-53 Pave Low helicopter for extraction from a live-fire exercise. The withdrawal is carefully coordinated to keep security in place until the Pave Low has lifted off. The AH-6 Little Bird and MH-60 (DAP) Black Hawk take gun runs on the smoking objective in case hidden pockets of resistance have survived. Door gunners on the Pave Low are ready to provide covering fire as well.

The large and powerful MH-47 Chinook helicopter provides transportation for Rangers to and from the objective. One Ranger said that the Task Force 160 pilots are the best taxi drivers on the block.

troops and direct action, including army Rangers. The MH-6 is a utility aircraft utilized to insert or extract small combat teams. Little Birds are capable of hot-weather, high-altitude flight. They boast the lowest maintenance-to-flight-hour ratio in the special operations aviation fleet. Equipped with forward-looking infrared (FLIR) sensors, the AH-6 can cruise at speeds of 260 kilometers per hour, and the MH-6 Little Bird has a maximum speed of 280 kilometers per hour. The helicopter's pilots have a choice of five secure radio networks, including one satellite communications network (SATCOM), to communicate with one another, with ground troops, or with commanders aboard naval ships.

Mission-enhanced Little Bird (MELB) AH-6 helicopters can carry an extensive armament for a specific mission depending on that mission and the helicopter's variant. Mission equipment updating includes lightweight planks, strap-on/off technology, a lightweight Hellfire missile system, and an integrated weapon management system. The lightweight planks provide not only a universal mounting platform for weapons, but mounting for external conformal fuel tanks and an external capacity for personnel.

The MH-53M Pave Low IV is a J-model that has been modified with the interactive defensive avionics system (IDAS)/multi-mission advanced tactical terminal (MATT). The system enhances present defensive capabilities of the Pave Low. It provides instant access to the total battlefield situation through near-real-time electronic order-of-battle updates. It also provides a new level of detection avoidance with near-real-time threat broadcasts over the horizon, so crews can avoid situations, defeat threats, and modify plans en route if needed.

With the AH-6's crew of two, the mission-enhanced Little Bird holds no passengers within its fuselage but boasts an armament of 7-shot or 12-shot 70mm Hydra rocket launchers, M134 7.62mm miniguns, MK19 40mm grenade launchers, and air-to-air Stingers. The miniguns are capable of firing 1,980 rounds per minute. A 30mm chain gun can be fired at rates of up to 750 rounds per minute. The AH-6 can be configured with other armament options, including 2.75-inch rockets, Hellfire laser-guided missiles, a 30mm cannon, and a .50-caliber machine gun.

To provide air support as mobile as the Rangers, the AH-6J special attack aircraft was developed. Based on a small, two-seat civilian helicopter similar to the military's OH-6A Cayuse, the AH-6J version fits aboard a C-130 cargo plane and can be unpacked and ready to fly five minutes after arrival. Its standard armament includes 2.75-inch rocket pods and Gatling-type 7.62mm miniguns.

The MH-6's principal task is transporting special operations forces into tight situations. The troops ride on two "planks" that are attached to the aircraft's sides, enabling the Rangers to disembark immediately upon reaching their destination. It requires a flight crew of two and accommodates a passenger load of up to six. This light utility helicopter has a maximum wartime infiltration radius of 518 kilometers. The MH-6 does not routinely accommodate its own armament, but instead relies upon the individual Rangers' artillery. In accordance with the MELB programs, artillery can be mounted on its external planks if necessary. The enhanced and upgraded MH-6 includes structural modifications that enable a maximum takeoff weight increase to 2,367 kilograms. This elevated weight allowance accounts for the crew, weapon systems, empty 65-gallon range-extension auxiliary fuel tanks, toolboxes, personal gear, mission cargo, the Rangers themselves, and the standard fuel capacity of 202 kilograms.

The mission-enhanced Little Bird (MELB) program upgraded the rotors, engine, and transmission systems; expanded the fuel tanks; and improved the structure of the AH-6 and MH-6. These Little Birds have been deployed in Grenada, Panama, the Persian Gulf, Desert Storm, Somalia, and other places, some that are classified direct actions. It was the AH-6s and MH-6s that prowled the streets of Baghdad during Desert Storm. These upgrades and extended capabilities were key elements in the assault and seizure of Panama's Torrijos-Tocumen International Airport and the Rio Hato Military Airfield during Operation Just Cause. SOCOM

BLACK HAWK

The Sikorsky-made MH-60A Black Hawk has evolved into three separate varieties: the MH-60G, known as the Pave Hawk and used by the U.S. Air Force Special Operations Wings; the MH-60L and MH-60K, both utilized by the 160th SOAR(A). The MH-60 variants of the original Black Hawk are the army's medium-sized utility helicopter. The Black Hawk variants were among the first equipped with the forward-looking infrared (FLIR) sensors, "disco light" infrared (IR) jammer, global positioning system (GPS), auxiliary fuel tanks, infrared suppressive exhausts, satellite communication (SATCOM), radar warning receivers, 7.62mm miniguns, and other numerous, cutting-edge special operations technological features. The MH-60-series helicopters can operate from a fixed land facility, remote land site, or ocean vessel.

Introduced in the late 1980s, the MH-60L was only about halfway through its operational evaluation when Iraq invaded Kuwait. The upgrade process was accelerated, and several of the L models were able to serve in Operation Desert Shield and Operation Desert Storm alongside the original MH-60A Black Hawks. No matter the variant or upgrade, Black Hawks serve the Rangers as utility helicopters for transportation of equipment, infiltration or exfiltration of troops, and close-combat air support during hostile operations.

The MH-60L's upgrades include aerial refueling capability, electronics such as color Doppler weather radar, Kevlar ballistic armor, and the capability to carry Hellfire missiles. A new folding tail simplifies use aboard naval ships. The MH-60K is the high-end special operations helicopter saturated with advanced avionics. In addition to the many upgrades on its earlier L model, the MH-60K features a fully integrated glass cockpit with custom-designed

Rangers from the 2nd Ranger Battalion prepare to disembark from an MH-6 Little Bird from the 160th Special Operations Aviation Regiment (Airborne). The MH-6 Little Bird carries four Rangers to a rooftop to clear the buildings during a training operation at Fort Bragg, North Carolina.

liquid-crystal displays for easier use with night-vision goggles. The MH-60K flight deck is designed for flying fast and low at night and in nearly zero-visibility types of weather. It has terrain-following radar and a forward-looking infrared (FLIR) sensor that provides complete weather information combined with map-of-the-earth information to enhance pinpoint navigation despite adverse conditions. A laser range finder allows the crew to detect, identify, and engage targets at an extended range with laser-guided missiles. Technologically advanced laser-guided Hellfire rockets are mounted on either side of the craft's body on detachable "wings."

The Black Hawk direct-action penetrator (DAP) version serves as an armed escort and fire support for Rangers and other special operations forces units. Accordingly, this variant is equipped with integrated fire control systems and pilot's heads-up display (HUD) that result in highly accurate and effective firepower. The 160th SOAR(A) pilots designed the DAP version with possible weapons configurations of two 19-round 70mm rocket pods, two 7.62mm miniguns, two forward-firing 30mm chain-guns, Hellfire rockets, and Stinger missiles.

An external hydraulic hoist system can lift 600 pounds with up to 200 feet of cable for rescue operations. Mounted on the helicopter's underside, a cargo hook is capable of supporting an external load of 9,000 pounds. An RSOV is attached to the external cable by a sling and transported by the Black Hawk to be dropped at a new location.

The fast-rope infiltration/exfiltration system (FRIES) quickly delivers large numbers of Rangers from rotary-wing aircraft, such as the Black Hawk and Chinook helicopters and Little Birds if necessary. The infiltration portion of this action is frequently referred to as fast roping. It is much like sliding down a firehouse pole, although this "pole" is a 40-, 60-, or 80-foot length of thick composite nylon rope, with the soldier's gloved hands acting as the brake. Rangers fast rope from helicopters with or without equipment, and they fast rope into water, onto fields, onto rooftops, or wherever they need to go.

During military operations in urban terrain (MOUT) training exercises to prepare Task Force 160 pilots and the Rangers they support, Little Birds engage practice targets with blank fire. The 2.75-inch folding-fin aerial rocket has a variety of special-purpose warheads. Its two M261 rocket launchers are mounted to either side. The miniguns provide voluminous gunfire at a rate of 2,000 to 4,000 rounds per minute.

Soldiers from A Company, 1st Battalion, 75th Ranger Regiment, deployed to Fort Campbell, Kentucky, take part in fast-rope training with the 160th Special Operations Aviation Regiment (Airborne). Fast roping is an expedient method of placing numerous Rangers onto a small objective. SOCOM

The fast-rope insertion/extraction systems (FRIES) mounted on either side of the aircraft's body can support 1,500 pounds each. The DAP Black Hawk can carry 12 to 15 Rangers and their equipment over 750 miles without refueling.

CHINOOK

The MH-47 Chinook and its variants are the 160th SOAR(A)'s long-distance, heavy-lift cargo helicopters. The fast-rope rappelling system, aerial refueling capability, and extensive avionics are similar to the MH-60K's system. The technological features give this heavy aircraft the unique capability to perform long-range flights despite harsh weather conditions, limited visibility, or low ceilings. The MH-47E holds 1,000 gallons of fuel in its internal fuel tanks, giving it the greatest flight range without refueling of any army helicopter. Chinooks routinely fly six-hour missions. The Chinook possesses the same glass cockpit as the MH-60K Black Hawk to enhance nighttime navigation. The 160th SOAR(A) pilots can fly the weighty MH-47 Chinook fast and low to the ground. The Chinook's air crews are specifically trained to provide armed close air support (CAS) and guidance for precise target engagement to support Rangers and other special operations forces. Weapon systems in three stations increase the aircraft's lethality. The left forward window and right cabin door each have 7.62mm Gatling-type miniguns, and the rear ramp mounts an M60 7.62mm machine gun.

The expansive cabin provides 42 cubic meters of cargo space and 21 square meters of cargo floor area. The Chinook can carry two high-mobility multipurpose wheeled vehicles (HMMWVs) or a single HMMWV with 105mm howitzer and gun crew. The interior permits the Rangers to transport their vehicles and drive the vehicles directly off the rear ramp upon landing. The cargo area can easily hold Zodiac rubber boats for water operations, and the ramp serves as the launching pad. The main

AH-6s were the first army helicopters in combat in Grenada in October, 1983. Six of the Little Birds were rolled from C-130s at the Point Salines airfield and were promptly photographed by wire services. One gunship was shot down supporting United States troops in daylight during the invasion of Grenada.

This agile helicopter serves as a multipurpose aircraft. During Operation Just Cause in 1991, an AH-6 crashed in a street and skidded through the Panamanian command headquarters entrance where the sentry on duty immediately surrendered to the two crewmen. All three were evacuated by an armored personnel carrier.

cabin can hold 33 to 55 fully equipped troops depending on the seating arrangements and special operations equipment. The Chinook can transport 24 litters and two medics. It requires a crew of two pilots and can accommodate a combat commander; a crewman operates each of the three weapons stations.

The Chinook has a triple-hook system for large external loads. Hooks are mounted to the Chinook's belly, with the central hook rated to carry up to 12,000 kilograms and the other two hooks rated to carry 7,500 kilograms each. These hooks can be used together to stabilize one heavy load or transport three separate loads.

The minigun has a range of 100 to 750 meters. The rocket pods can be used as a point target weapon between the ranges of 100 and 750 meters, and as an area fire weapon of up to a 7,000-meter range.

PAVE LOW

The MH-53J Pave Low is the U.S. Air Force's heavy-lift, long-range special operations helicopter. First deployed in 1981, the MH-53 airframe and avionics have been continuously and extensively upgraded to expand the aircraft's operational capabilities. The Pave Low helicopter performs missions in heavily defended airspace during night and adverse weather conditions. Missions include search-and-rescue coverage, infiltration, exfiltration, and resupply of special operations forces. When vertical takeoff and landing are required, the Pave Low's upgrade, MH-53J Pave Low IIIE, answers the call.

The Pave Low's flight range reaches 630 miles with added external fuel tanks. Its range is unlimited with aerial refueling. It can fly up to altitudes of 16,000 feet and less than 100 feet above the ground. Low-altitude maneuvers are made possible by technological advances such as terrain-following and terrain-avoidance radar, a forward-looking infrared sensor, satellite communication (SATCOM) radios, and a global positioning system (GPS). A projected moving map display enables the crew to follow terrain contours and avoid obstacles. This navigational system allows the Pave Low to fly at night without detection and arrive on target at the precise time. It can travel at speeds of 165 miles per hour at sea level.

Rangers board an MH-47 Chinook helicopter for a fun jump. This type of training is usually conducted without combat equipment and weapons. The large and powerful MH-47 Chinook helicopter carries special operations vehicles like Zodiac rubber boats, ground mobility vehicles (GMVs), and motorcycles.

Four Rangers are extracted by a Black Hawk helicopter. The Task Force 160 pilot must immediately gain altitude for the safety of the Rangers below. Each Ranger is secured to the line by a body harness and two locking snap links. Upon reaching the desired destination, the Black Hawk hovers and they unhook one at a time.

A C-17 drops Rangers during a mass tactical jump with combat equipment. The Rangers from the 75th Ranger Regiment jump from the C-130, a propped aircraft. They also jump from a C-141, a jet aircraft.

This 42,000-pound helicopter is equipped with radar-warning receivers as well as chaff and flare launchers to help defend the aircraft from enemy missiles. The Pave Low can be armed with up to three 7.62mm miniguns or .50-caliber machine guns for suppressive fire. Extensive armor covers the vital areas of the aircraft to increase crew and passenger serviceability. Maximum passenger capacity is 38 troops or 14 litters, and the craft can sling up to 20,000 pounds with its external cargo hook. Flight training for the Pave Low takes about eight months to complete. Operation of this helicopter requires extensive knowledge and carefully coordinated teamwork. The aircraft requires two pilots, two enlisted flight engineers, and two aerial gunners. In search-and-rescue missions, two U.S. Air Force pararescue medics accompany the crew.

C-130 and C-141

The U.S. Air Force Special Operations Command's C-130 Hercules performs the tactical portion of an airlift mission. Versions of the C-130 perform airlift support, Antarctic ice resupply, aeromedical missions, firefighting duties for the United States Forest Service, and natural disaster relief missions. In relation to Rangers and special operations forces, the C-130 is the transport for mass tactical airborne insertion and air dropping equipment into hostile areas. Using its aft loading ramp and door, the C-130 can accommodate a wide variety of over-sized cargo, including but not limited to Little Bird helicopters, utility helicopters, six-wheeled armored vehicles, and HMMWVs. Palletized cargo is dropped from

Rangers fill the sky in a mass tactical jump from an air force C-17. The Rangers only jump during daylight hours for training purposes. While jumping onto an enemy objective, the cover of darkness helps conceal the Rangers and gives them a tactical advantage.

Rangers spill forth from a C-130 in a mass tactical jump at a 1,500-foot altitude. All Rangers are airborne qualified and learn how to gain control over their parachute canopies and guide their parachutes by pulling toggles to direct themselves toward the drop zone (DZ). They also know how to handle parachute malfunctions like twisted risers or partially inflated canopies.

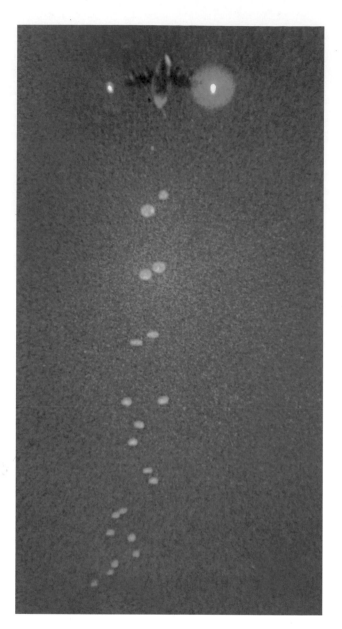

Under the cover of darkness Rangers from 1st Battalion jump onto the "rock" drop zone, the active runway at Hunter Army Airfield that is so large that it acts as a secondary landing site for the NASA space shuttle. The men on this jump are exiting from a C-17 and are jumping from an altitude of 1,500 feet.

Daylight jumps are rare for Rangers in the regiment. Night conceals air operations and helps achieve the element of surprise. The Ranger is most vulnerable when sitting in an aircraft rigged up and floating to the ground. The dark night sky hides them as they drift to the drop zone.

aircraft along with the Rangers. For water operations, a ranger squad, with its combat rubber raiding craft (CRRC), parachutes into the water from a C-130 aircraft. The C-130E/H/J variants can hold 74 litters, 92 combat troops, 64 paratroopers, or a combination of these. The C-130J-30 version can accommodate 97 litters, 128 combat troops, 92 airborne troops, or a combination of these.

The desert mobility vehicle (DMV) rolls off an air force C-17 and prepares to move to a link-up point with other DMVs. An entire patrol of fully equipped desert mobility vehicles and accompanying Rangers is accommodated by the vast cargo interior of this aircraft.

The C-130 aircraft can air drop loads of up to 42,000 pounds. It uses high-floatation landing gear to land and deliver cargo on rough dirt strips. The Hercules C-130E and C-130H variations require a crew of five: two pilots, navigator, flight engineer, and loadmaster. The C-130J and C-130J-30 versions require two pilots and a loadmaster.

The C-141A, built between 1963 and 1967, was air mobility command's first jet aircraft designed to meet military standards as a troop and cargo carrier. The C-141B Starlifter is able to airlift combat forces over long distances; deliver those forces and their equipment either by air, land, or air drop; resupply forces; and transport the sick and wounded from the hostile area to medical facilities. Within the cargo compartment, the C-141 can transition from rollers on the floor for palletized cargo, to a smooth floor for wheeled vehicles, to aft-facing seats or sidewall canvas seats for passengers in order to accommodate different missions. This mammoth aircraft is crewed by two pilots, two flight engineers, and one loadmaster, with the addition of one navigator for air drops. It can transport 200 troops, 155 paratroopers, 103 litters and 14 seats, or 68,725 pounds of cargo.

The massive C-17 aircraft can transport several fully loaded ground mobility vehicles (GMVs) in a roll-off mode. Larger aircraft, like the air force's C-5, can transport an entire ranger patrol of fully equipped GMVs.

Rangers swiftly move onto their objective during a raid. Tracers light up the night sky so bright that starlight becomes obscured. The support element pours firepower on the objective until signaled to "lift and shift" off those targets so the assault element can remove them altogether. Little Birds firing 2.75mm rockets prepare and soften the objective prior to the Rangers' assault.

SPECTRE

The AC-130 Spectre gunship has a combat history dating to Vietnam-era "puff" gunships. The present-day U model is the third generation AC-130 gunship. The AC-130H/U gunships' primary missions are close air support, air interdiction, and force protection. The AC-130U is designed to bring enormous firepower in support of ground forces. While the earlier variations simply saturated whole areas with projectiles, the new aircraft uses state-of-the-art sensors and fire-control equipment to steer its 105mm howitzer and 25mm and 40mm cannons with great precision. The sensor suite consists of a television sensor, infrared sensor, and radar. These sensors allow the gunship to visually or electronically identify friendly ground forces and targets in any place and at any time. This weighty aircraft can reach speeds of around 300 miles per hour at sea level. The AC-130U has a crew of five officers (pilot, copilot, navigator, fire control officer, electronic warfare officer) and eight enlisted (flight engineer, TV operator, infrared detection set operator, loadmaster, and four aerial gunners). When a Ranger makes a call for fire, he just may be calling in Spectre.

Static lines are rigged to each Ranger prior to leaving the aircraft. This attached line deploys the parachute from its pack. Rangers receive their airborne training early in their careers and must perform jumps at regular intervals to remain qualified. Rectangular chutes are easier to control than the circular or dome-shaped chutes, and are deployed by a rip cord on high-altitude low-opening (HALO) jumps.

Support Elements and Vehicles

Each ranger battalion has a support element for home station training. This unit (riggers, truck drivers, maintenance, etc.) is not organic, but through individual post memorandums provides the battalion with the necessary requirements to meet mission/training demands. It is important to note, however, that this unit does not deploy with the battalion, although it is responsible for supporting the ranger force's outload for combat. The logistical and support arrangements for extended support remain a constant ranger concern.

Above: **Moving down a highway in desert mobility vehicles (DMVs) in Iraq, Rangers ready themselves for any possible action or improvised explosive device (IED) that may be waiting down the road. The DMV can easily transport nine or ten fully equipped Rangers and their food, water, fuel, ammunition, missiles, and other weapons. Navigational and communication systems specific to a Ranger's mission requirements are standard on the DMV. When loaded and ready to roll, the DMV can weigh 13,500 pounds.** SOCOM

Left: **A ground mobility vehicle (GMV) can carry 10 Rangers fully loaded with combat equipment comfortably and with every man but the driver pulling a sector of fire. In Afghanistan, however, as many as 14 Rangers fit onto one of these vehicles moving from point to point.** SOCOM

Ranger units have a limited antiarmor capability (84mm Carl Gustav and Javelin) and lack organic indirect fire support (60mm mortars only). The Stinger is the only air defense artillery (ADA) system. Ranger units have no combat support (CS) or combat service support (CSS) and deploy with only five days of supplies. There are no organic transportation assets. As a result of the lack of CSS, ranger units require logistical and mission support from other services and/or agencies. Ranger battalions are light infantry and have only a few vehicles and crew-served weapons systems.

The Special Operations Support Command (Airborne), SOSCOM, was activated on November 1, 1995, as the newest major subordinate unit in the U.S. Army Special Operations Command. Its activation realigned the command-and-control organizational structure of the following units: 112th Special Operations Signal Battalion (Airborne); 528th Special Operations Support Battalion (Airborne); Material Management Center (Airborne); and five special operations theater support elements (SOTSE). This organizational structure concentrates support for all U.S. Army special operations forces units with dedicated and regionally oriented combat and health services, communications planning, overall coordination, and a liaison base. SOSCOM is located at Fort Bragg, North Carolina.

This reorganization left a SOTSE in each of five geographical regions around the world. The SOTSE soldiers are embedded in theaters' army staff. They plan

Today's ground mobility vehicles (GMVs) have specialized tires that resist punctures and deflating and can withstand extreme hot and cold. A specialized swing arm on these special operations vehicles supports the 240G machine gun facing the vehicle's rear.

M1025A2 "Heavy Hummer"

Max speed: 65 miles per hour
Max load: 2,375 pounds
Standard length: 15.5 feet (185.8 inches)
Height: 6 feet (72 inches)
Width: 7 feet 1 inch (85inches)
Curb weight: 5,326 pounds
GVW weight: 7,700 pounds
Configuration: 4x4
Ground clearance: 1 foot 4 inches (16.1 inches)
Wheelbase: 10 feet 9 inches (129.5 inches)
Track: 71.6 inches
Suspension: Four-wheel independent double A-arm, coil spring
Fuel capacity: 25 gallons

and coordinate with theater army, SOSCOM, and special operations forces, including the Rangers, to ensure support during operations and training. As army staff members, these officers and noncommissioned officers have knowledge of theater-specific requirements and capabilities that assist units in coordination with the theater of operations.

The Material Management Center provides the Rangers and special operations forces with centralized and integrated material management of property, equipment maintenance, logistical automation, and repair parts and supplies.

Specializing in advanced communications and resupply capabilities, members of the 112th Special Operations Signal Battalion (Airborne) and the 528th Special Operations Support Battalion (Airborne) have a challenging mission supporting the Rangers. In their respective fields, signal and support soldiers provide supplies, maintenance, equipment, and expertise, allowing special operations forces to "shoot, move, and communicate" on a continuous basis. Because the Rangers use equipment unique to their missions, soldiers assigned to the 112th and 528th units are taught to operate and maintain a vast array of specialized equipment not

The predecessor to today's ground mobility vehicle (GMV) was used during Operation Iris Gold with the Kuwaiti military to provide close-support services in the event of another invasion. Following the experiences of Desert Storm, special operations forces units, including the ranger battalions, began investigating options beyond the ranger special operations vehicle (RSOV). The need for a specialized long-range patrol vehicle for a desert environment was evident. The possibilities of modifying the existing military vehicles were investigated, and the standard high-mobility multipurpose wheeled vehicle (HMMWV), or Humvee, answered the call. SOCOM

The early ground mobility vehicle (GMV) was a modified high-mobility multipurpose wheeled vehicle (HMMWV) with additional machine gun mounts and the team's radios, weapons, and enough fuel and supplies to operate in the desert for 10 days. GMVs are also known as desert mobility vehicles (DMVs). The DMV is the special forces' version of the HMMWV, tailored for long patrols in the desert environment. This DMV carries fuel and water supplies, soldiers' rucksacks, an M240G machine gun, and a Browning M2 .50-caliber heavy machine gun, plus all communications and navigational systems.

A ground mobility vehicle (GMV) moves from an objective after conducting a training mission with Task Force 160 at Fort Campbell, Kentucky. These Rangers are from the 1st Ranger Battalion based at Hunter Army Airfield, Savannah, Georgia. Rangers frequently train with their support elements since these same units will support them during deployments to Afghanistan and Iraq.

With the best night-vision equipment available, the Rangers use AN/PEQ-2 infrared pointers and illuminators to spot enemy targets and illuminate the battlefield. These beams of green light are only seen by members of the regiment using night-vision goggles such as the AN/PVS-14s. SOCOM

Below: **Each Ranger on the ground mobility vehicle (GMV) is assigned a sector of fire, a specific direction and area to supervise for enemy action. These rugged vehicles withstand the harshest conditions of mountains, rivers, swampy bogs, and desert sands. Each has mounts for weapons like the M240G and the M2 .50-caliber machine guns.**

Above: **Ground mobility vehicles (GMVs) have special markings to identify them as friend or foe. At the top of the antenna is an infrared light with special tape that can only be seen with night-vision goggles. On the sides of the door marked with an "X" another symbol identifies the vehicle and its soldiers. The desert mobility vehicle (DMV) has an infrared headlight mounted in the middle of the grill so the driver can see the road ahead while wearing his night-vision goggles.** SOCOM

These Rangers are on patrol in a ground mobility vehicle (GMV) during a mission in support of Operation Enduring Freedom (OEF) in eastern Afghanistan. The flat valleys are encircled by rugged mountains, possibly hosting Taliban observational outposts. SOCOM

normally used by other units in the armed forces. To meet the needs of the Rangers, the two battalions have developed logistical and signal platforms that are deployable on a moment's notice. Rangers are on the move, and their support elements must be as well. Soldiers assigned to the 112th and 528th units are airborne qualified.

The 112th Signal Battalion integrates the theater of special operations command (TSOC) attached to each TSOC at their home stations. When deployed, the 112th establishes communications elements at the forward operating base (FOB) level and at the Joint Special Operations Task Force (JSOTF) level. The ranger units

provide the spokes of the communications network, but the 112th provides the hubs. The hub is crucial as it then connects to the satellite for global positioning.

RANGER SPECIAL OPERATIONS VEHICLE (RSOV)—A THING OF THE PAST

The ranger special operations vehicle (RSOV) was a modified Land Rover that was introduced after the first Persian Gulf War. Impressed with its vehicular capabilities, the

Rangers from the 1st Ranger Battalion conduct armed reconnaissance along a route believed to have been used by Osama bin Laden in the Lowgar region of Afghanistan. SOCOM

Rangers initially purchased 60 of these vehicles, affording a minimum of 12 to each ranger battalion. The main purpose of the RSOV was to provide the Rangers with a mobile defense capability. Produced by British-based Land Rover's special-vehicle operations, these did not serve as assault vehicles, but as a method for rapidly applying forces to key locations in the Rangers' fast-paced battlefield. RSOVs were useful in establishing battle positions that provided the Rangers some standoff capability for a short duration, such as during an airfield seizure mission.

Designed for a minimum crew of three, the RSOV required a driver, gunner, and leader or second gunner. Maximum capacity was a six- to seven-man crew. Within the ranger regiment, the RSOV's primary battlefield function was as weapons carrier, medical vehicle, or communications vehicle. Based on the 110 Land Rover chassis, the RSOV was powered by a four-cylinder turbocharged engine

with plenty of power and torque for hauling loads around the battlefield's rough terrain. As a weapons carrier, it accommodated up to 8,000 pounds of ammunition and six fully armed Rangers. It was compact enough to fit inside a Chinook or a C-130 cargo plane and could be sling-loaded underneath both Chinook and Black Hawk helicopters.

The RSOV mounted a M240G machine gun and either a MK19 grenade launcher or M2 .50-caliber machine gun. There was also a mount for a machine gun in the passenger-side seat and the capability for the passenger to operate an antiarmor weapon such as the RAWS, Javelin, LAW, or AT4.

RSOV platoons were also equipped with a number of military motorcycles. From 1988 to 1995, the Rangers relied on the Honda CR250. In 1996, they switched to the Kawasaki KLR250, which is used today, along with a newer bike based on the Suzuki DS80. One of the chief attractions

The Klepper Kayak

The Klepper is an Eskimo-styled and German-engineered kayak made of a folding wood frame and a pliable but durable covering. It folds into one bag for storage or transportation. The average assembly time for one person is 20 minutes without tools or force. Disassembly takes approximately five minutes. Generally powered by paddles, it can glide silently at 5 miles per hour. The military "Commando" version weighs a little over 80 pounds with an estimated payload of 850 pounds.

Advancing Technology

Rangers are afforded with the most technologically advanced weaponry and communications systems available worldwide. Rangers operating in Afghanistan have encountered difficulties communicating with Task Force 160 pilots and with each other due to the mountainous terrain. Small, lightweight, hand-held computers assist with overcoming communications obstacles. The Intel X-scale 500+ MHz processor uses satellites that enable over-the-horizon communications, an integrated Global Positioning System (GPS), and Blue Force tracking to map the battlefield. Each device is networked so that all soldiers are working with the same information. Use is simplified by a color LCD touch screen. From this computer, a Ranger can send messages, request support, map the area, and use information provided by other Rangers in the system to plan movements. Should this hardware fall into enemy hands, the Ranger can clear its information by remote command.

of this smaller bike is that it can be palletized more easily and dropped from aircraft along with the Rangers.

GROUND MOBILITY VEHICLE (GMV)

The special operations command is always looking for methods and machinery that will improve the overall effectiveness of the ranger battalions. A ranger unit can only be effective if it's in the right place at the right time. For mounted ground operations, mobility, capacity, and sustainability of the ranger teams are crucial for a successful operation. The GMV, or ground mobility vehicle, has become the vehicle of choice, especially over the past decade in the vast desert environments of the Middle East.

The HMMWV, or Humvee, entered army service in 1985, and was designed to replace the M151 series of jeeps as the United States military's primary troop- and cargo-carrying lightweight truck. The Humvee is a highly mobile, diesel-powered, four-wheel-drive vehicle equipped with an automatic transmission. Humvees are designed for use on all types of roads and terrains and in all weather conditions. Using various common components and kits, the HMMWV can be configured to become a troop carrier, armament carrier, sheltered carrier, ambulance, TOW missile carrier, or a scout vehicle.

The predecessor to today's GMV was used during Operation Iris Gold with the Kuwaiti military to provide close air support services in the event of another invasion. The early GMV was a modified HMMWV with additional machine-gun mounts and the team's radios,

weapons, and enough fuel and supplies to operate in the desert for 10 days. The GMV is also known as the desert mobility vehicle, or DMV. The DMV is the special forces' version of the HMMWV, tailored for long patrols in desert conditions. Extra fuel and oil filters are installed to prevent damage from fine sand and dust. The DMV was first deployed during Operation Desert Storm and was used by army special forces for patrols along the Saudi borders with Iraq and Kuwait and some missions behind Iraqi lines in Kuwait.

The GMV began life as a standard M1025A2 Heavy Hummer manufactured by AM General, headquartered in South Bend, Indiana. With the support of the Letterkenny Arsenal near Chambersburg, Pennsylvania, and the U.S. Army's Tank-Automotive and Armaments Command (TACOM) at Picatinny Arsenal, the vehicle has been modified and is still evolving to meet the needs of the Rangers. The present-day GMV began as the basic M1097A2 Humvee, and was upgraded to Model M1113 as an expanded-capacity vehicle (ECV) with a 190-horsepower, high-performance 6.5-liter turbocharged diesel engine. The M1113 Hummers are equipped with heavier frames, strengthened power trains and braking systems, and heavy-duty wheels and tires designed to carry heavier payloads without sacrificing the vehicle's mobility and

Rangers in a ground mobility vehicle (GMV) ford a river during a mission in support of Operation Enduring Freedom (OEF) in Afghanistan. The GMV has a ground clearance of 16 inches. SOCOM

Ranger platoons are equipped with a number of military motorcycles. The Kawasaki KLR250 is used today, with the addition of a newer bike based on the Suzuki DS80. One of the chief attractions of the smaller Suzuki is that it can be palletized more easily and dropped from aircraft along with the Rangers.

The Suzuki DS80 motorcycle is small enough to be jumped from aircraft and attached to the side of MH-6 Little Birds for rapid deployment and direct action against the enemy. More maneuverable than the desert mobility vehicle (DMV), the DS80 has improved suspension, noise-reduction exhaust, and is mounted with an infrared headlight that can only be seen by personnel wearing nods, or night-vision goggles. The bikes are also painted infrared black to help conceal them while in action.

performance. State-of-the-art electrical systems enhance the vehicle's dependability. Extra fuel and oil filters prevent mechanical and engine damage from fine sand and dust incurred in desert environments. The GMV has a 16-inch ground clearance despite its low silhouette, which makes it a very stable vehicle that is hard to roll over.

The GMV-specific armament modifications for the ranger units include swingarm mounts for the M240G 7.62mm machine gun and a heavy mount for either the M2 .50-caliber machine gun or the MK19 40mm automatic

grenade launcher. Also included are mounts for an array of four-round smoke grenade launchers. The GMVs have enhanced radio and satellite communications gear, improved ballistic protection, camouflage nets, an electric winch, a Blue Force tracking/positioning locator, and a GPS receiver. This specialized vehicle has vast storage for food, water, fuel, ammunition, missiles, and other weapons, and accommodates four to five fully equipped Rangers in addition to its required crew of two. The standard weapons load includes M4 carbine and M9 9mm

Motorcycles are quick and maneuverable transportation that are mostly used for administrative and security purposes. Each can transport two riders and can be used to secure a road leading to an objective. A special bracket is mounted over the Kawasaki KLR250's handlebars to accommodate the Ranger's weapon.

pistols as personal weapons systems, M24 and XM107 .50-caliber sniper systems, AT4 rockets and, added more recently, a supply of the Javelin antitank missiles. When fully loaded, the specially transformed Humvee can easily tip the scale at 13,500 pounds or more.

The GMVs can be air dropped to an area of operation by parachute on a specialized pallet, located, and driven away by the airborne-inserted Rangers. A loaded GMV fits into the cargo compartment of an MH-47 Chinook if the suspension is compressed, but it is a tight squeeze.

The massive C-130 aircraft can transport several fully loaded GMVs in a roll-off mode. Larger aircraft like the air force's C-17A Globemaster can transport an entire team of outfitted GMVs.

ZODIAC

Rarely does the Zodiac see action these days, with the diminished need for water transportation in the desert and mountainous environments of Iraq and Afghanistan.

This all-terrain vehicle is another asset to the Rangers' transportation, and each ranger company is allotted five. The ATV has a variety of uses, such as moving wounded men and equipment, building objectives in training environments, policing personnel or equipment on a drop zone, and bringing chow to the men. It is mostly used for administrative purposes. Equipped with winches in both the front and back, it can be easily shackled down inside an aircraft for deployment.

However, the Zodiac is routinely used in training and during the Florida phase of Ranger School.

For water operations, the Zodiac landing craft can be paddled, or an engine can be mounted at the rear for amphibious assaults. These rubber boats are ideal for ranger special operations. They have flattened hulls and shallow drafts that allow for greater accessibility through shallow rivers, waterways, low wetlands, and swampy areas. The Zodiac's design also permits landing at sites not accessible to conventional boats, such as beaches, river banks, marshes, and coral reef flats. Another feature that makes this craft especially useful for the Rangers is its six air-filled compartments connected by valves, which allow the regulation of internal air. So the Zodiac will float even if one (or several) compartments deflate. These specialized air compartments boast the weight-carrying abilities to support a squad of Rangers and their equipment. When necessary, several Rangers can grab the carrying handles and portage the craft for limited distances.

Paddling down the Nisqually River near Tacoma, Washington, 2nd Battalion Rangers are tactical and stealthful without the use of outboard motors. Zodiac rubber boats have flattened hulls and shallow drafts, which allow for greater accessibility through shallow rivers, waterways, low wetlands, and swampy areas. Six air-filled compartments connected by valves allow the internal air pressure to be regulated. The Zodiac will float even if one or several compartments become deflated.

Rubber raiding boats can sit fully loaded in the cargo area of an MH-47 Chinook. The aircraft glides along the water's surface and lowers the back ramp. Rangers push the Zodiac out and follow it, get in, and start paddling. The same boat can be secured to the belly of an MH-60 Black Hawk or pitched out partially inflated to deploy Rangers in other situations. A squad and its Zodiac can parachute into the water from a C-130 aircraft. As soon as the Rangers splash down, they swim like mad to the watercraft. Then they fire up the boat's specially silenced 35-horsepower outboard and head for land, guns trained on the shoreline. Rangers have cleverly named such water operations "rubber duck ops."

The Individual Soldier

In the days of the Holy Roman Empire, soldiers bore a shield and carried a sword or spear. As our nation laid its foundation, Revolutionary and Civil War soldiers armed themselves with a hatchet and a rifle, and possibly a few dozen rounds of ammunition. They traveled light with only a canteen, wool blanket, and minimal food provisions. The modern light infantryman's load is anything but light in comparison to his forebears. Armed with a fully automatic

Above: The trick is to be flexible. Most Rangers can adapt to any change in plans, so during the 2004 Best Ranger Competition the participants were tasked with firing a bow and arrow with a goal of hitting a target 25 meters away to receive points for the event.

Left: The tomahawk throw was a surprise event at the 2004 Best Ranger Competition. Each Ranger was given three practice throws and then moved to the graded test. The competition was organized by buddy teams so the team chose who participated in which event according to each individual's strengths. No prior knowledge of these events was conveyed to the participants. Competition organizers like to incorporate weapon systems not commonly utilized by Rangers.

rifle, hundreds of rounds of ammunition, and various grenades, the infantry soldier is ready for whatever he encounters. He also has night-vision optics and radio communications. His load increases as he dons his protective body armor and helmet. And to sustain the modern infantryman, water, food, and medical kits accompany each individual.

The individual infantry soldier is the central component to any offensive or defensive military action. It's the soldiers on the ground that win wars. The U.S. Army has embraced the concept of the individual soldier as the military's most important weapon system. Viewing the individual soldier as a weapon system requires comprehensive examination of every functional aspect of the soldier. This focused examination encompasses the surrounding supports and points to the individual warrior that makes things happen. The ranger battalion is outfitted with its own support element, transportation, and weaponry according to specialized operational requirements to address the soldiers' needs to accomplish the mission. The elite and highly skilled individual Ranger is also outfitted with his own specialized ballistic protection, clothing, and equipment to provide optimal fighting capabilities in any environment and under any condition.

The Department of Defense has increased the size of the special operations community by adding over 3,900 personnel from FY 2004 to FY 2009. This growth primarily supports the staffing requirements to wage a global war

The modular integrated communications helmet (MICH) is the only ballistic helmet used by the special operations command that's authorized for use with motorcycles and all-terrain vehicles. Most importantly, it protects Rangers from flying bullets. The ballistics are rated to stop a 9mm bullet traveling at 1,450 feet per second, from 0 degrees of obliquity (straight on, with no angle), with a high degree of survivability. The bolts used to hold the suspension onto the shell are ballistic, and the bolts must pass the same ballistic tests as the helmet shell itself. This is important, because other ballistic helmets currently available have non-ballistic hardware in place. If an incoming round strikes a bolt head, it would send a secondary projectile (the bolt) into the soldier's head.

on terrorism. The individual special operations forces soldier remains the key element to success in special operations missions worldwide. The needs of the combat-mission Ranger and the solutions to such needs are ever-changing, as today's technology rapidly replaces itself with more innovative, creative, and successful options. Advanced technologies entering and leveraging special operations missions for the ranger regiment

include the ability to access, identify, and neutralize all types of conventional explosives, ordnance, and impro- vised explosive devices (IED), an ominous threat in Afghanistan and Iraq. Ranger missions benefit from the technologies used to collect timely intelligence and to enable sustained dissemination of crucial intelligence, information, and communication in denied-access areas or hostile situations.

Rangers do not jump while wearing their ranger load carrying system (RLCS). The RLCSs are placed in an assault pack or rucksack and put on after de-rigging from the parachute. A waist belt (or sub belt) that is part of the RLCS is worn when jumping and has pockets for two 30-round magazines for combating any enemy as soon as the Ranger hits the ground. After placing the weapons into operations, Rangers will pull their RLCS out of their packs and suit up for the mission.

Special operations forces equipment advanced requirements' (SPEAR) body armor/load carriage system (BALCS) consists of body armor, an equipment load-carrying subsystem, and a backpack subsystem. Featuring the latest advancements in state-of-the-art technology, Bianchi International and Gregory Mountain Products have developed the ultimate backpack system for the twenty-first-century warrior. Designed to meet the stringent field requirements of the U.S. Army Rangers and special forces, this system combines superior load-bearing technology with advanced backpack design and offers a modular system capable of efficiently carrying up to 120 pounds of equipment for urban, jungle, desert, mountain, or arctic warfare. The BALCS maximizes ballistic protection, buoyancy compensation, and load-carrying capacity, while minimizing the burdens of weight, bulk, and heat stress. Rangers carry all of their equipment, supplies, and provisions required for the mission and resupply is highly unlikely. Portions of

the pack can be removed if not needed, thus reducing unnecessary weight and adapting it to a variety of uses.

Each component subsystem is readily compatible with the others. The lightweight body armor provides protection against fragmentation, handgun, and rifle threats. The armor system contains a soft armor vest, front and back interchangeable upgrade plates, and modular neck and groin protection. The previously issued Kevlar personnel armor system ground troops (PASGT) vest, also referred to as a flak jacket, did not meet the Rangers' needs quite like the ranger body armor (RBA) with specifically designed ballistic body protection consisting of a flexible vest and a rigid plate. The flexible RBA vest has a Kevlar filler with a camouflage nylon fabric exterior that can protect the front and back torso from most 9mm rounds. It weighs approximately 8 pounds in comparison to the weighty 25-pound flak jacket. The 8-pound rigid ceramic upgrade plate provides additional front torso coverage when inserted into the front pocket of the vest. Its aluminum-oxide ceramic construction of 2x2-inch tiles

continued on page 115

Above: **The new Rhodesian assault vest is the best load-carrying equipment to be introduced since the commencement of the global war on terrorism. The vest can hold 16 30-round M4 magazines. It has an integrated hydration system on the back and can be fitted with level-4 body armor.**

Left: **This Ranger has newly issued equipment that's ready for deployment to Iraq and Afghanistan. The ranger load carrying system (RLCS) has pockets for communication equipment like digital radios, a GPS navigation system, a first aid kit, and magazine pouches. Everything the Ranger needs is easily within his reach.**

The ranger load carrying system (RLCS) has a pouch under the American flag for accessories such as a flashlight, maps, and a small notebook. Behind this panel is space for a body armor breastplate on the front and back. Pouches are set according to the shooter's preference. The only thing that is standard is the placement of the first aid pouch, which is found, when facing the Ranger, on the lower right-hand side. The special forces communications system (at right) was designed according to specific Ranger requirements. Due to its sophisticated engineering, radio communications remain unaffected by high-noise situations. This system provides quality communication with active hearing protection.

The CamelBak on-the-move hydration system was initially introduced to the athletic community by a cyclist who had nearly caused a big crash when he reached for his water bottle during a race. At an after action review (AAR) following a training mission, Rangers hydrate with their CamelBaks, now standard-issue equipment. Canteens are a thing of the past.

Eye protection keeps foreign debris, especially fine grains of sand and blinding winds in Iraqi deserts, out of Rangers' eyes. The lenses are shatter and scratch resistant.

Below: **The lensatic compass is designed to make exceedingly accurate bearings for land navigation and directing artillery fire. It is comprised of a compass card (rose), degree scale and rotating bezel, sighting wire unit/top cover, thumb hook, and lens. To take a bearing or azimuth, the Ranger opens the top cover halfway to a 90-degree angle with the compass card. He then lifts the lens arm up to roughly a 45-degree angle with the thumb hook down and a thumb placed into the hook for stability. Looking at the targeted object, he positions the sighting wire in the middle of the object. Moving the lens up and down enables the Ranger to read the fine degree markings from the card without taking his eyes off the object. The bearing reads in degrees or mils.**

"Lead by example and your men will follow." At the end of the lane, the Rangers will be expected to engage targets while their heart rate is racing from all the physical activity; lack of food and sleep are also adding to the stress.

The MK46 5.56mm machine gun, modular information communications helmet (MICH), and Wiley X protective eyewear are ready for engagement. The helmet has a bracket on the front for mounting night-vision goggles and Velcro on top for special tape to signal to friendly aircraft. The weapon system is topped with a white light tactical light and an AN/PEQ-2 laser pointer and illuminator. The Trijicon advanced combat optical gun sight (ACOG) 4x scope rounds out a very deadly weapons system.

Energetically will I meet the enemies of my country.

The quintessential Ranger is geared up to complete the mission, although he may be the lone survivor. His equipment makes him complete: M4A1 rifle with advanced combat optical gun sight (ACOG) 4x32 power scope, AN/PEQ-2 infrared target pointer/illuminator/aiming device, M203 grenade launcher, modular integrated communications helmet (MICH) headgear, and lightweight internal communications equipment. A ranger squad leader leads his men by example.

"I believe the ranger regiment's greatest success over the past year has been the ability to transition from sustained combat operations in Afghanistan back to decisive combat operations in Iraq, back to sustained combat operations in both Afghanistan and Iraq without a period of recovery," said Colonel James Nixon, ranger regimental commander. "Over the last year, the ranger regiment has conducted combat operations with almost every deployed special operations force, conventional and coalition force in both Afghanistan and Iraq. It has also continued to recruit, assess, and train the next generation of Rangers and Ranger leadership." Over 70 percent of Rangers have conducted multiple combat deployments, and many are on their fifth or six rotations since 9/11.

protects an approximate 10x12-inch area from 5.56mm and 7.62mm rounds. The inserts can be removed quickly and easily when not needed. An optional overvest can be worn with the ranger body armor to provide additional protection to the back torso against small arms and fléchette rounds. The body armor system of the BALCS replaces the ranger body armor.

The equipment load-carrying subsystem (ELCS) is the modular pocketing and harness system (H-harness or vest styles) that allows for specific configuration tailoring of the individual's equipment load and weapons system for any mission. The ELCS comes in one size and features easy adjustments for shoulder, waist, and chest. The backpack subsystem is a modified commercial backpack subsystem comprised of a backpack, patrol pack, and butt pack. To a Ranger, this glorified backpack is called a ruck or rucksack. Once the Ranger is geared up, his weapons and equipment can weigh anywhere from 70 to 100 pounds. The backpack's state-of-the-art internal frame affords a stable platform sufficient to carry 120 pounds effectively. The backpack efficiently transfers the load from the shoulders to the waist and provides adjustment straps to fit the significant majority of Rangers, despite physical size. The butt pack and the patrol pack can attach to the ELCS harness or vest without the backpack component. These can also be worn with the backpack.

Rangers frequently use the patrol pack as their "assault pack," a compact and lighter weight pack to carry ammunition and supplies for a brief mission of 10 hours or less. The backpack subsystem weighs 17 pounds when empty. Load capacity for the backpack is 120 pounds, the patrol pack is 50 pounds, and the butt pack is 13 pounds.

The ranger assault carry kit (RACK) is the current load-carrying equipment for all soldiers of the 75th Ranger Regiment. It can be configured for individuals according to their needs and military occupation specialties, from medics to radio operators to machine gunners. The RACK can be assembled in a host of configurations suitable for any mission environment. Rangers use components of the RACK to constitute an assault pack for their missions of limited duration. Since it is worn on the chest, it does not conflict with a waist belt. The RACK frees up the hips and abdomen areas. The RACK also helps protect the upper body from fragmentations, bullets, and trauma because it gets gear up on the chest area for extra protection. It can be worn with or without body armor.

The basic RACK begins as a chest harness with over 15 pouches of various sizes for customization. In the ranger battalion, one leg pouch is required on every Ranger's left thigh, and it must carry their personal emergency medical supplies.

Whatever the configuration, the rucksack includes an

Above:**Rangers use different radios for different missions. The AN/PSC-5 working in conjunction with satellite communications (SATCOM) allows Rangers to talk with command group. The AN/PSC-5 is a multi-band man-portable communication radio (with ultrahigh frequency/very high frequency) capable of satellite communications.**

Right: **The Rangers rely on the 112th Signal Battalion to establish a communications hub that transmits intelligence and information from troop to troop and troop to commander. Communication computers are miniaturized for individual soldier use in the field.**

Left: **Placing the AN/PRC-148 radio into operation is a graded task for the expert infantryman's badge (EIB). Rangers are masters at all infantry tasks. It is these skills and determination that will make the Ranger successful on the battlefield.**

B Company Rangers prepare to jump on a drop zone in South Carolina. The wind speed and direction are given to the aircraft to be passed on to the jump masters in the bird readying the rigged Rangers.

The Panasonic Toughbook is the ranger regiment's standard computer. Older versions of the computers were similar to Commodore 64s and are now completely obsolete. These rugged new computers are needed to interface with advanced navigational and communication systems in Humvees, aircraft, and individual radios.

The Panasonic Toughbook laptop computer interfaces with an AN/PSC-5 radio, manufactured by the Raytheon Company, giving it satellite communications (SATCOM) capabilities.

Communication is one of the most mission-essential aspects of any successful military operation. The Rangers train on an AN/PRC-124 radio during expert infantryman's badge (EIB) testing.

on-the-move hydration system—a backpack-style water bladder with a self-sealing drinking tube. Most infantry commanders have allowed soldiers to use their personal CamelBaks in training prior to the army's more recent widespread adoption. Presently, each Ranger is issued a CamelBak (the most common manufacturer of this system) for on-the-move hydration, and Rangers have readily adopted the name in reference to this canteen

replacement. The canteen may be one of the oldest icons of army life, but infantry officials would rather equip soldiers with a hands-free drinking system. For decades, soldiers have depended on canteens as their primary means to carry water into battle. Except for the switch from aluminum to plastic, the basic design hadn't changed since 1910. Cumbersome 1-quart canteens are now considered obsolete.

Depending on the mission, combat soldiers usually carry 4 to 6 quarts of water in the field, which previously meant two 1-quart canteens and one or more 2-quart canteens mounted on each hip in snap pouches, on the rucksack, or carried inside. The CamelBak hydration system has a 2- to 3-liter insulated plastic pouch with a long, flexible straw that fits over the Ranger's shoulder and clips to the front, allowing him to easily rehydrate whenever needed. It is possible to carry a 100-ounce

I will never leave a fallen comrade.

As Rangers prepare to execute their objective, medics and headquarters personnel ready the wounded for extraction and medical transport. A medic pulls a wounded Ranger on a Skedco stretcher. This pliable and durable plastic stretcher becomes rigid when the injured is secured inside. When not moving the wounded, the Skedco can be used to remove important pieces of equipment from the objective area. Attachable straps and handles allow for pulling along the ground, horizontal hoisting by helicopter, or vertical hoisting in confined spaces. Weighing less than 20 pounds, it compactly stores in a large pack. The platoon sergeant and first sergeant position themselves at the tail end of the helicopter's ramp to count personnel and maintain accountability of every Ranger. No one is left behind.

pouch in the rucksack, another 100-ounce pouch in the attached patrol pack, and a 70-ounce pouch on the back, totaling about 8 liters of water. The on-the-move hydration system permits the Ranger to keep his hands on the weapon and his eyes focused on the objective. The human body can lose more than 1 liter of water per hour during intense physical activity. If water is not replaced, dehydration can cause heat stress, headaches, nausea, fatigue, and even temporary loss of muscle endurance and short-term memory.

The special forces communications system was designed and engineered according to the specific requirements of special operations forces like the Rangers. The communications system was designed for interoperability with a military aviation intercom and various military field radios. A Ranger can use just one headset whether in an aircraft or on the ground. Due to sophisticated engineering, radio communications remain unaffected by high-noise situations. This system provides quality communication with active hearing protection. Maintaining peripheral hearing is crucial to any mission, and the ability to amplify potential warnings enhances the safety of the individual and the unit. This system provides electronic hearing protection that can amplify ambient sounds and promote hearing safety in up to 110-decibel environments. The communication system's noise-attenuating boom microphone performs in exceptionally loud environments. The hearing protection blocks out the noise of nearby artillery while amplifying communications between Rangers. Two AA batteries provide up to 250 hours of operation. Radio communications are not lost or compromised because of battery loss due to two independent audio channels.

The specialized modular integrated communications helmet (MICH) combines unmatched ballistic protection with improved communications capabilities. Several varieties are available, including the TC2000 and TC2001 combat helmets and TC2002 close-quarters battle (CQB) gun fighter helmets. The helmet's single-piece design eliminates the use of non-ballistic bolts, which, if hit by incoming ammunition, can injure the individual. The MICH helmet allows for maximum visual and aural sensory awareness for the user. The helmet accommodates night-vision devices, combat communications systems, protective ballistic

A young ranger squad leader with a face of determination and fatigue looks over the condition of his men before moving on. Communication is paramount to the overall success of a ranger operation, as is apparent by the two AN/PRC-148 inter-squad radios.

A ranger squad leader directs the assault element to the objective during a blank-fire exercise. He carries an M4 carbine with a double stacked magazine. Rangers rehearse training missions with blank rounds before training with live rounds. Gillian M. Albro, USASOC PAO

eyewear and goggles, oxygen masks, and nuclear, biological, and chemical (NBC) protection.

Without communications systems, the MICH helmet weighs approximately 3 pounds. The MICH has a pad foam suspension system that, after a short period of time, conforms to the shape of the individual soldier's head. The higher cut of the helmet allows the Ranger complete range of motion and unobstructed field of view while wearing the body armor/load carriage system (BALCS). It permits a user to crouch or lie prone and engage a target, a very difficult task with the old personnel armor system ground troops (PASGT) helmets,

Rangers wear a Velcro American flag on their right shoulder as most American troops do. When conducting operations in enemy territory, a Ranger will remove the American flag for security reasons. In combat environments, ranger uniforms are equipped with a name tag, U.S. Army tape, and rank. Other identifying unit insignia is restricted.

body armor, and load carriage/load bearing equipment. The pad suspension system provides impact protection for airborne infiltrations, including static line and free-fall airborne operations.

The standard infantry PASGT helmet has a one-piece construction of multiple layers of Kevlar 29 fabric. The helmet provides ballistic protection for the head, neck, temples, and ears. The helmet was adapted for the ranger and airborne units and includes the parachutists' impact liner (PIL), a thick foam pad that provides impact protection and a specialized chin strap that maintains the helmet in position during airborne operations. The helmet weighs about 3 pounds.

One of the Ranger's greatest weapons is the element of surprise, so the cover of night is an opportune time to initiate a mission. Night vision is essential, and the lightweight AN/PVS-7D night-vision goggles meet the Rangers' need. The night-vision goggles, commonly referred to by Rangers as "nods," are worn on the head and over the face and are held in place by head straps. The straps allow for one-handed mounting and dismounting. A binocular eyepiece assembly incorporates an infrared light source and amplifies existing ambient light to provide illumination, permitting greater visibility for night operations. Night-vision goggles are designed to work in conjunction with rifle-mounted aiming sights, and they provide an optimal viewing distance of 150 to 350 meters and a focusing range of 25 centimeters to infinity. The nods have a field of view of 40 degrees, weigh 1 1/2 pounds, and operate for up to 50 hours on two AA alkaline batteries.

Once exhaustion sets in, the next Ranger will take over and drag for a while. A 3rd Battalion company squad leader leads the way by dragging a 250-pound dummy on a stress-fire course. "Train like you fight," said one ranger officer overseeing today's training event. The officer was deployed to Afghanistan twice and was preparing to return once again.

The AN/PRC-148 radio is comprised of a receiver and a transmitter. The radio has approximately 2,320 channels and includes voice and digital communication. The operating voltage for the radio is 13.5 volts from the primary battery. It has a range of 5 to 10 kilometers on high power based on line of sight and location, weather, and surrounding noise level. The AN/PRC-126 radio is more lightweight and best utilized for squad operations. The radio-telephone operator in the squad or platoon frequently carries this portable radio. Today's Ranger is equipped with a small and lightweight individual radio with a control that straps to the wrist and an earpiece and microphone. This eliminates the need to pull the radio from a rucksack during intense operations.

Rangers, special operations forces, and Task Force 160 pilots in Afghanistan have found that signals between their GPS navigational equipment and satellites in space may be blocked by the 10,000-foot or higher surrounding mountains. For this reason, the Rangers continue to train to use the altimeter, which measures height, as a back-up to GPS. The altimeter is preferred to the compass, as the compass requires dead reckoning and counting paces—very difficult to implement accurately in mountainous terrain.

In 1974, the black beret was the authorized headgear for the Rangers to wear with their battle dress uniforms and dress uniforms. Rangers of the 75th Ranger Regiment received official authorization through AR 670-5, Uniform and Insignia, January 30, 1975. Previously, locally authorized black berets had been worn briefly by certain ranger and LRRP companies during the Korean and Vietnam Wars. Armor and armored cavalry personnel wore black berets as distinctive headgear until Command Sergeant Major of the Army Bernard W. Rogers banned all such unofficial headgear in 1979. In October, 2000, Army Chief of Staff General Eric K. Shinseki announced that black berets distinctive of the 75th Ranger Regiment would be the army's standard headgear beginning June 14, 2001. Special operations and airborne soldiers could continue to wear their distinctive colored berets; soldiers in army airborne units wear maroon berets, and army special forces soldiers wear green berets. In response to this change in the dress code and desiring to remain visually distinctive from other service member and units, with the approval of General Shinseki, the 75th Ranger Regiment adopted the tan beret beginning in June 2001.

The battle dress uniforms (BDU) are issued as utility, field, training, and combat versions. Their camouflage pattern is designed for jungle, wooded, desert, or arctic environments.

The Ghillie suit accessory kit (GSAK) items are packed in a flyer's kit bag and assembled by snipers and long-range surveillance personnel when they attend their respective training courses. The kit also provides Rangers with the various camouflage components needed to construct, repair, and modify Ghillie suits to meet mission and climatic requirements. Soldiers will custom make each suit to their own design and performance requirements. The kit consists of jute burlap strips in four colors; duck cloth; nylon cord; sewing needles and thread; foam padding; tie straps; over-white trousers, mittens, and parka; camouflage face paint, netting, and covers; and several other accessories. Natural colors, patterns, and textures are incorporated into the materials to replicate the landscape's indigenous qualities. To enhance the dimensionality of the camouflage ensemble and break up the outline of the body, a ranger sniper will cover his arms, back, and helmet with natural vegetation. It is not uncommon for a Ranger to attach clumps of brush, twigs, leaves, or plants as part of the camouflage process, as not every Ranger is afforded a Ghillie suit kit.

Snipers low crawl, high crawl, and observe noise and light discipline as they stealthily approach their position. Local vegetation helps the sniper blend with the natural surroundings. Snipers learn camouflage techniques and design their own Ghillie suits to disguise their presence in specific environments. Ghillie suits were developed by Scottish game wardens during the 19th century to catch poachers. The belly or front side of the Ghillie suit is smooth and absent of pockets so the sniper's clothing will not snag on the ground while crawling. It also helps with fluid, quiet movement. Moving from one position to the next, foliage in the Ghillie suit is repositioned to hide the sniper's silhouette. Concealed in teams of two, the snipers are silent and deadly.

Come rain or come shine, a Ranger is out in the weather. A lightweight rain suit of Gore-Tex is the standard protection from the wind and rain. The waterproof parka has a drawstring hood and double front closure. The trousers have a drawstring waist and adjustable elastic ankle cuffs. Both parka and trousers stuff compactly into their own pockets.

The Ka-Bar combat fighting survival knife with a fixed 7-inch blade dates back to World War II. Many members of the United States Armed Services depend on this basic weapon. Many Rangers also depend on the Leatherman-type compact multipurpose tool. Made of stainless steel, this tool requires minimal maintenance to prevent rust and corrosion. Its design is a flat square or rectangle with tools neatly tucked inside for immediate access to knives, pliers, wire cutters, Phillips-head and flat screwdrivers, bottle/can opener, scissors, and a fingernail file.

Index

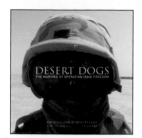
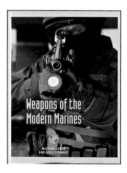
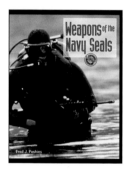

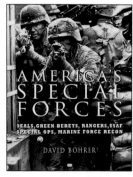

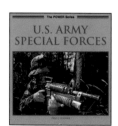